Make Your Kid a
Millionaire

**Eleven Easy Ways Anyone
Can Secure a Child's
Financial Future**

Kevin McKinley

A FIRESIDE BOOK
Published by Simon & Schuster
New York   London   Toronto   Sydney   Singapore

FIRESIDE
Rockefeller Center
1230 Avenue of the Americas
New York, NY 10020

FIRESIDE and colophon are registered trademarks
of Simon & Schuster, Inc.

Designed by Christine Weathersbee

Manufactured in the United States of America

1   3   5   7   9   10   8   6   4   2

Library of Congress Cataloging-in-Publication Data
McKinley, Kevin, date.
Make your kid a millionaire : eleven easy ways anyone can secure a
child's financial future / Kevin McKinley
p.   cm.
1. Parents—Finance, Personal.   2. Finance, Personal.
3. Estate planning.   I. Title.
HG179 .M384   2002
332.024'01—dc21   2001040853

ISBN 0-684-86564-5

For information regarding special discounts for bulk purchases,
please contact Simon & Schuster Special Sales at 1-800-456-6798 or
business@simonandschuster.com

Acknowledgments

This book reflects the good fortune that I have had in my life. I am incredibly lucky to have been a part of the lives of so many good, decent, and intelligent people.

Despite their best efforts, more teachers have put *up* with me than have educated me. But Jim Bilot and Wanda Meinen inspired in me a love of numbers that borders on the abnormal. Ken Ripp, my high school economics teacher, and Diane Lindstrom, at the University of Wisconsin, taught me about how money influences the things people do, and I am thankful for their dedication to their profession.

I also learned more about tax and legal issues from an hour with Sam Stagliano and Sam Geraci, respectively, than I could have in a whole semester of business classes.

Thank you to Kathy Sahlhoff, the financial aid expert at the University of Wisconsin-Eau Claire.

Thank you to Ev Anderson for justifying the confidence Rachel and I have in you as a child-care provider, and for making our lives easier.

Thank you to the C.V.S. for their friendship, fun, and good food.

Thank you to the Adlers for bestowing a tremendous honor on Rachel and me.

Thank you to Mike and Marty O'Halloran, for serving as family friends, role models, and clients. And my sincere appreciation to Teresa for never "sugarcoating" it—that's what makes her opinion valuable.

I owe a tremendous amount of gratitude to the clients I have worked with over the past thirteen years, and I am honored by the trust they have placed in me. Although *I* was paid to serve them, a few people have taught me priceless lessons about money, values, and family. Thank you, Jerry, Dick, Jean, Bill, and Tom.

Thank you to the experts at my firm for their advice and patience, specifically Ron, Keith, and Vicky. Thank you to Mike K. for backing me, and to Connie for hiring me so many years ago.

They say everybody's a critic, but a few people evaluated my work especially well. I thank Jill Basta and Sarah Thurs for their time and thoughts. And Beth Bornhoeft's technical skill, work ethic, and overall brilliance have already boosted my family's net worth, to say nothing of my writing skills and ability to deliver useful information.

Thank you to Mike Dieckman for the number crunching, and also for being a great friend. I am lucky to know him, and to be a witness to his honor, decency, and humor. He is a "man" in the best and truest sense of the word.

I am indebted to the good people I work with at my office for helping me accomplish my goals. Knowing Rita Campbell is wonderful, but working with her is even better. Her enthusiasm is contagious, and I thank her for her support, assistance, and encouragement.

Ron Farley, the best investment adviser I have ever known, sets the standard for hard work, ethics, and compassion, and I will enjoy watching him share that with the people he works with.

I can't give enough praise to my agent, Andrea Pedolsky, for her skill and expertise, and for believing in me, and this book. I also am indebted to her for introducing me to Doris Cooper at Simon & Schuster. Doris is a truly amazing person. I would be proud if my daughter turned out like her (I will have to fight Doris to make sure she leaves this in).

Thank you to my grandmothers, Gladys and Edithmae, for showing the rest of us how to live long, and live well.

Without my stepmother Nancy's encouragement, this book might never have reached the level it did. I thank her for making our family part of her own.

I am so proud of my sister, Mary, and my brother, Christopher, and I love you both as only a big brother could.

I love my mother Ann's spark, attitude, energy, and resilience, and am glad she is so close to Rachel, Ellie, and me.

My father Mike's support for this project has been overwhelming. I only hope I can bring as many lessons and as much laughter to other people's lives as he has.

I want to thank my daughter, Ellie, for making me feel the wondrous gift of love for a child that only a parent can have. The love she has given to me in return, in spite of all the hours I have spent working on this book, brings tears to my eyes. I regret having to leave her at home, and I promise to her that from now on, whenever she tells me, "Da Da, no work! Da Da, play . . . Ellie . . . *now!*" I will gladly be able to accept.

And finally, and most important, thank you to my wife, Rachel. You serve so well, in so many roles, for so many people. You have been heroic in your patience and strength. Your love for me has been a constant source of inspiration, and your presence in my home and heart fills me with warmth and joy. You are the person whom I most admire, and my best friend. I am truly blessed to be your husband, partner, and soul mate. You are beautiful. I love you, Rachel.

For Rachel and Ellie

Contents

Contents

Introduction

It's hard to justify spending an hour planning for something that won't happen for another ten or twenty years when you still have to make dinner, put tomorrow's lunches together, and figure out your holiday plans. And by the time you get the dishes, bath, and homework out of the way, and conquer the bedtime stalling tactics, you can barely think about what needs to be done by tomorrow, let alone in a few decades.

I understand.

The good news is that compared to the frenzied juggling that is part of most parents' lives, planning for your child's financial future takes less time and effort than figuring out how to get one kid to soccer practice and the other to the doctor (and back) all in the same afternoon. In fact, by taking just a few minutes to think about the available opportunities, you can give your child what all parents want for their children.

More.

More than what you have.

More money? Sure. But what you really want for your child are the things that more money can provide.

More time.

More freedom.

More knowledge.

More stability.

I know how you feel. This book came into being because of the hopes and fears I have for my child. In 1999 my wife Rachel and I were blessed with the birth of our daughter, Ellie. Right away our dreams and paranoia over our child's well-being went into overdrive. I remember taking our baby home from the hospital, cruising the interstate at a cautious twenty-five miles per hour, and scowling at every car that came within ten feet of our vehicle. I spent most of Ellie's first night at home hiding any sharp objects and barricading the door to the basement stairs.

Within a week I had mapped out who my daughter's friends would be, set some ground rules for dating, chosen her future college, and decided where she would eventually settle down (close enough so that I could see my grandchildren on a regular basis).

Rachel pointed out the futility of these activities and suggested I turn my attention to something that would actually help Ellie now: setting up an investment account for her.

Like most things Rachel says, this made sense. I could actually start doing something about Ellie's future.

By taking a few simple steps, Rachel and I could not only save ourselves money today and down the road, we could make Ellie's life more enjoyable, too.

And that's really what investing for your child is all about. When everything is said and done, ironically, *it's not about the money!* You already know that having a million-dollar net worth isn't, by itself, going to answer all of her prayers or guarantee her perpetual bliss. And I would guess that when you first picked up this book, you didn't have a vision of your child one day rolling around in a huge pile of hundred-dollar bills, giggling uncontrollably.

Your interest in your child's financial future is probably similar to why Rachel and I are investing for Ellie. What we envision for our child is a life of security, choices, and freedom.

We want her to attend her preferred college, regardless of the cost. If she decides to get married, we want her to marry someone for love, not money. When she chooses a career, we would like her to do so based not on how much money she can make, but on whether she'll honestly look forward to going to work each day. If she doesn't, she should have the freedom to change jobs or return to school without suffering from a drop in income.

We hope she can live in a comfortable house in a safe neighborhood with good schools, and be home enough to enjoy the company of her family and neighbors. If it is a priority for her family, we want her or her spouse to be able to stay home to care for their children (our grandchildren!) without worrying about the loss of cash flow.

That sounds pretty good, doesn't it? (If not, read it again while you imagine a full orchestral version of "God Bless America" playing in the background.)

But investing for a child is not only about making the good times great. It will also help avoid the terrible tragedies a lack of money can bring.

A recent poll sponsored by AARP showed that almost one in five respondents stayed in an unhappy marriage because the individual couldn't afford to live alone. Harvard professor Elizabeth Warren recently released a study of the 1 million personal bankruptcy cases that were filed during 1998. Despite being an expert in her field, even she was shocked to find out that almost half the people involved had some type of major illness or injury, and the subsequent medical expenses made the people insolvent. What is even more alarming is the vast majority of the people wiped out by these medical bills already had health insurance. But what they didn't have was a "cash cushion" to soften the hard landings life can bring.

By taking a few minutes out of your day to open this book, you have made the first step necessary to ensuring that a lack of money will never stand in the way of your child's happiness and well-being.

The Rewards

For Your Child

It's easy to see how investing for your child will give her material benefits. But the gifts she receives go far beyond the simple accumulation of money and even well past the goals of "freedom, choices, and security."

First of all, like most everything else in your child's life, you are the prime source of her education, both in what you say and what you do. And you can talk about the virtues of foresight, frugality, and denial of gratification until you're blue in the face.

But when you actually set up an account for her, you set an example. You are delaying little bits of short-term gratification now, in exchange for reaching big long-term benefits down the road. Strange as it might seem, by investing money for your child, you are demonstrating the exemplary behavior that could very well keep her from squandering the money.

And the lessons you are teaching are not limited to financial issues. Whether you are saving for your child's college education, first home purchase, or comfortable retirement, you have identified a goal. You have established a long-term plan to obtain that objective, and you won't be stopped until you've reached that destination. When your child eventually decides she wants to reach a particular goal on her own, your behavior has given her a blueprint.

Thinking today about your child's tomorrow will also give her a tremendous advantage over the children of parents who choose not to put any money aside. Quick experiment: two high school seniors, same intellect, work ethic, and background. One can afford to go to college (and does). The other can't, and enters the workforce immediately. Which kid do you think is going to have the better life? Be exposed to new ideas? Enjoy work more? Earn more money? Okay, saving for your child's future doesn't guarantee a life of quality, but it sure gives her a better shot at happiness than *not* doing anything.

For You

Investing for your child might seem like one more "labor of love" that we perform for our children. But taking the steps to secure your child's financial future will give you huge rewards, too.

You will first experience a payback at tax time. This book contains dozens of ways that you can use several investment vehicles to legally cut your tax bills, while at the same time increasing your family's overall net worth. It all boils down to whom you want to have your money: Uncle Sam or your child.

You will also benefit from being forced to reexamine your spending habits to decide what your priorities are. It's a natural progression of what we go through when we change our lifestyles to account for the responsibility of a child.

Before we became parents, our financial mistakes didn't hurt anyone but ourselves. Spent $200 on a pair of shoes? Eat ramen noodles for a month. Lost all your savings on a dumb stock tip? Hey, it wasn't that much money to begin with. An impromptu trip to Mardi Gras? Sure—put it on the credit card. Why save for the long term when the long term is a long way off?

Then a new, tiny person is thrust into our lives. She relies on us for everything, twenty-four hours a day (there's a reason she's called a "dependent"). All of a sudden our boneheaded money moves are taking food out of her mouth.

Once you decide to invest for your child, you are forced to look ahead to needs that will arise ten, twenty, even fifty years down the road. As you start examining how your money choices will affect your kid's future, you will realize just how many things you can do without today in return for a better tomorrow. You'll stop before each purchase and ask, "Is it worth it?" My guess is that more often than not, your answer will be, "No." And the money will stay in your pocket, where (like so much lint) it can't help but accumulate.

Investing for your child now will aid your retirement later. That sounds crazy, but it's not too far-fetched. Depending on your child's age, putting a few thousand dollars aside now may completely cover her college fund or retirement account. Once you make the deposit, you can sit back and let the power of time grow your child's wealth while you focus your investments and your attention on securing your "golden years."

Getting your child's financial needs out of the way now will not only help you accumulate money for retirement but also give you guilt-free enjoyment of the autumn of your life. Many retired people I've worked with accumulated a decent-sized nest egg by the time they were ready to stop working. But some of them were hesitant to spend the money on anything beyond the basic necessities of life. When I would ask them why, many told me that they wanted to leave something for their children, and they were worried they might outlive their money!

By putting aside just a few dollars today, you can one day blow your wad on a condo in Boca with no fear of condemnation from your kids.

Tax breaks, increased frugality, and the ability to completely focus on your own financial goals are enough to motivate just about anybody to take action. But the intangible yield can be even more inspiring.

First, you are going to experience peace of mind like you won't believe. Shortly after Ellie was born, I had a dream that she was eighteen years old, and ready to go to college. But when I told her that I didn't bother to save any money for her, she just furrowed her brow and stared up at me in disappointment (for some reason, in the dream she was still two feet tall), not saying a word. I woke up in a cold sweat, and the next day opened her college savings account.

That's one nightmare I don't have anymore.

You'll also enjoy the satisfaction of knowing you've done the right thing for your child. And that pleasure will only grow along with the dollars, until it culminates with you handing the money to her at the appropriate time.

And that's really when you'll receive the ultimate reward: your child's appreciation and gratefulness for your foresight and discipline.

What Do You Need to Make Your Kid a Millionaire?

You already have the three most important tools needed to secure your child's financial future: a lot of your love, a little bit of money, and this book.

And that's about it. You certainly don't have to be a millionaire to make your child one. As a matter of fact, research shows that four out of five American millionaires are the first ones in their family to reach that level of wealth.

You don't have to be an investment wizard, either. You only need the same level of intelligence necessary to accomplish typical financial tasks. Things like paying taxes, buying a car, and getting a mortgage. If you've done any of these in the past, you can start your child on the road to financial independence.

You do need to spend a few hours reading this book. Lock yourself in your bedroom. When your kids start pounding on the door and screaming your name, you are perfectly justified in yelling back, *"Leave me alone! I'm trying to make you a millionaire!!"*

But once you finish the book, you don't need to spend a lot of time watching the tech stock television channels or reading the financial section of the daily newspaper, either. We're talking long-term goals. Short-term news won't affect you, so paying attention to it won't do any good. You can quit surfing the Web, and go play outside with your kid instead.

You do need a little discipline. But not "Marine Corps" discipline. Just enough to get going on the steps that make the most sense for you and your family. It's the same self-motivation that gets you to the supermarket each week so that your family doesn't starve.

And you will need to be flexible. There will be obstacles on your child's path to financial independence. People change, new laws appear, and fresh opportunities arise. But reviewing your situation for a few hours once a year—I like to do it around tax time—is more than enough scrutiny.

How Do You Get Started?

Investing for your child is a journey. Unlike many trips that involve our children, this one lasts a long time *and* it's enjoyable. This book will serve two purposes for your trip. First, it is a guide to reaching your overall goal of your child's financial independence. It chronologically maps out the steps you should consider at each stage of your child's life, from her birth to your death.

Second, each of the eleven investment chapters provides a discussion of a particular vehicle that can help you and your child reach a specific destination. The background, benefits, and drawbacks of each method are presented to help you decide which approach is best for you and your family.

Set Your Goals and Choose Your Vehicle

As with any trip, first determine where you're going by deciding what you want to achieve for your child. Protecting your kid if you're not around? Definitely. Paying for college? Probably. Funding a comfortable retirement for her? Who wouldn't want that? Helping her buy a home? Hey, it might prevent her from moving back in with you.

Once you have established your destination (or destinations), you can decide what means of transportation and routes are the best ones to get you where you want to go. And when you are investing for your child, you will find that a single investment can be applied toward several different objectives, and an objective can be reached by using several different investment vehicles.

Funding Your Vehicle

An exciting feature of investing for your child is that you can harness the full strength of the most powerful ally of savers and investors: time. The more time you have, the less money you need. It helps to consider the connection like a seesaw:

Time   Money

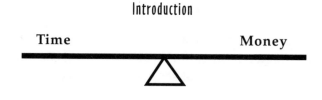

Childhood development experts tell us that much of how we turn out as adults is determined by the time we are two years old. I like to take that one step further and say that we have the power to form our children's financial futures, especially by taking action in the first few years of their lives.

If you want to make your child a millionaire in ten years, you need to deposit almost $400,000 today in an account earning 10% annually. But if you have fifty years, you only need about $8,500. And if you have enough money today, you can even make a single deposit into the vehicle appropriate for each one of your goals and be done with it.

How much should you put in? That depends on a few variables, including the rate of return your money earns, taxes, and the rate of inflation (both in the rise of prices in general, and in the cost of your particular goal). Unfortunately, nobody knows what those numbers are going to be in the future.

But you can make projections using different hypothetical figures. For instance, let's say that you want to make a deposit today so your child can go to college in eighteen years. You would need to know the following numbers:

1. The cost of the college education today (let's say $40,000).
2. How much that cost will rise each year (guess about 5%).
3. At what rate your money will grow (figure 10%).

Once those numbers are in place, you can determine that you would need to deposit about $17,000 today.

How did I come up with that figure? I used my trusty Texas Instruments BA-35 Solar calculator. I love it so much that I get jittery if it's not within arm's reach at all times. You can buy it or one like it for about thirty bucks, or you can use the online calculators that most financial service and mutual fund companies provide on their Web sites.

I could just about hear you groan as you read "$17,000."

Whenever anyone tells you these kinds of scary numbers, it makes you want to stick your fingers in your ears and sing "La la la" out loud until the person drops the subject. Especially if, like most of us, you don't have these big sums of money just lying around doing nothing.

But, of course, you have an alternative to securing your child's financial future through one big deposit. You can make several little ones. Time helps this method of investing, too, as the more time you have, the more little deposits you can make. You don't have $17,000 right now to fund your kid's college costs? Fine. Start saving a little over $5 a day at the same rate, and you'll still get there.

And best of all, by saving money in little, regular steps, you won't miss it. I've helped hundreds of people set up systematic programs to save for their retirement, or their children's futures. At almost every initial meeting, the client hems and haws when I ask him what he's going to set aside. He's thinking, "I'm barely getting by now. Where am I going to come up with another few hundred dollars a month?" I assure him that he won't even notice the money being taken out, but he doesn't believe me. Finally, I point out that he can always reduce or even eliminate his contribution if he wants to.

Over the last thirteen years, I can think of only a handful of people who reduced the deposit amount, and just a couple who eliminated it altogether. But almost all of the other people have told me that after a month or two, they don't miss the money one bit!

Another interesting thing happens to you when you start and maintain a program of regular saving. By the time you have accumulated enough money to fund your goal, you'll realize that you still don't need the amount that was going toward your systematic investing plan. You will have the luxury of pointing your ongoing deposits toward another investment goal.

Where Is the Money Going to Come From?

"Okay, Kevin, we've set the goals, and we have lots of time on our side until the goals need to be reached. There's just this one teensy-weensy little obstacle left before we can secure our child's financial future: *we don't have any extra money!!!*"

Yes, you do. You have tons of money that you spend every month. It's just a matter of deciding what your priorities are, and where your child's future ranks in relation to those expenditures. Should you shut off your electricity so that you can put a few hundred dollars a month into a mutual fund? No. That would be more traumatic to your child than not having money for college tuition. And you should probably continue to pay your taxes, as even a short-term prison sentence would deprive you and your child of each other's company.

The average American employee works about three hours out of every eight just to pay taxes. Yet that same worker can make a kid a millionaire in fifty-three years by investing just *five minutes* of wages each day at a 10% annual return.

But you do have something called "discretionary spending." That is money that isn't going out for necessities, but it's still going out. And the road to your money goals (including your child's financial independence) goes right smack-dab through that discretionary spending.

Many times people will call me and say, "We make a decent living, but we can't seem to find any money to invest. Can you help us out?"

I sure can. But the solution is a lot like good exercise: it hurts a little while you're doing it, you are relieved when it's over, and afterward you are the better for it.

Showing Yourself the Money For one month, write down all the different ways, down to the last penny, that money leaves your household: taxes, groceries, mortgage, car payments, credit card payments, everything. If you throw a nickel into a fountain for good luck, it goes on the list, too.

At the end of the month, take a sheet of paper and divide it into three columns. (If you have something like Quicken for your computer, this will be even easier.) Make a list of all the expenses on the left side of the paper. Put the largest at the top, and the smallest at the bottom.

Then sit down with a calculator, and start at the top of the list. Go over each item. Ask yourself, "Is this item absolutely crucial to our existence?" (Note: If you are married, you are fortunate to have a person in your household who will be more than happy to give you plenty of feedback regarding the frivolous expenditures you make on your behalf. If he or she is like my wife, this may even be something of a hobby.)

If you can't possibly survive without the item, leave it on the left-hand side for the time being. If you can exist without it, write the amount in the middle column. Do this for the rest of the list. After you get to the bottom, total up the numbers in the middle column.

You now have a sum that is probably several hundred dollars, and it represents the source for the funds necessary to secure your child's financial future.

But you don't have to give up all of these creature comforts. This isn't about living like a *Survivor* contestant just so your kid can go to Harvard. However, you do need to decide what you can forgo now so that your financial goals for your child can be realized.

If you still can't come up with anything, you can use what I call the Painful, Powerful Prioritization Process. Just go through the middle column line by line and make this statement (out loud) each time: "Spending $143 per month on my cell phone is more important to me than sending my child to college." Or "Having my nails done professionally means more to me than making my child financially independent."

If you can speak the words out loud without laughing at the absurdity, keep the item in the middle column. If your self-respect disappears before you finish the sentence, sheepishly move the item to the column on the far right.

If you are doing this exercise with your spouse (and you should), it can quickly degenerate into a "Your-stupid-ways-of-wasting-money versus my-stupid-ways-of-wasting-money" confrontation. You may want to agree in advance that each of you will reduce your own discretionary expenses by an equal dollar amount or percentage.

When you're done, your paper will look something like this abbreviated example:

Expenses		Nonnecessities	Can Live Without
Income taxes	$2,114		
Mortgage pmt.	943		
Property taxes	318		
Food	750		
Salon appts.	150	$150	
Golf lessons	250	250	
Cell phone	140	140	$140
Eating out	250	250	250
		Total	$390

By the time you total up the numbers in the right-hand column, you will have more than enough money to start saving for your child's benefit.

And the opportunity is not confined to just your regular monthly expenses. I like to run three or four times a week (I figure it's a cheaper stressbuster than alcohol or psychotherapy). Although I live in an area with some spectacular running trails and paths, I began lusting after a $2,000 high-performance treadmill about the time Ellie was born. Rachel and I could have easily afforded it, and I had made all kinds of mental justifications as to why I "needed" it: it's my only vice, I could run at home, any time of the day, health reasons, blah, blah, blah.

But about the same time as I was deciding which one to buy, I made the calculation that $2,000 could make Ellie an after-tax millionaire by the time she turned sixty-five. I tried to follow through with purchasing the treadmill, but my heart just wasn't in it anymore. Now Ellie has $2,000 in her Roth IRA (in Chapter 8 you'll find out how I achieved this), and I'm still running outside. Wisconsin winters can make this a pretty chilly form of exercise, but I am warmed by the thought of making my daughter financially independent.

The dollar amounts don't have to be this dramatic to make a difference. Any time you're contemplating a purchase of anything over a few hundred dollars, or you have a daily expense of a few dollars, stop for a minute. Pick up a calculator and figure out what the cost of this splurge will be today, and what the money earning 10% annually might buy for your child in twenty, thirty, or fifty years. This chart might help you:

Dollars and Time	One-Time Deposit	or Daily Saving
$10,000 in ten years (a semester's expenses at a public university)	$ 3,855	$1.60
$50,000 in twenty years (a year of college at a private school)	7,432	2.15

$250,000 in thirty years (a small starter home)	14,327	3.59
$1,000,000 in forty years (at 3% inflation, over $300,000 in today's dollars)	22,095	5.12

It's your business what you spend your money on. Rachel and I have cable Internet access at our house, along with about a dozen premium channels. Our monthly bill is starting to rival our mortgage payment. You might think that we are wasting our money on this, and most sane people would agree. But we don't go to movies in theaters, and we tape a lot of the movies to watch together after Ellie goes to sleep.

And we feel we have enough money working toward our financial priorities. If you are in the same situation and you feel you have enough money to meet the long-term financial goals for you and your child, spend away.

But if you are feeling too strapped to follow any of the investment ideas in this book, you need to at least stop for a second and examine what is important to you. If you take that inventory of where your money is going and still find you can't possibly make a change, fine. At least you tried. But my guess is that you will discover hundreds of dollars each month going down holes that, in the long term, rank near the bottom of your priority list.

It really comes down to this: Do you want to have a little bit of stress now, or a lot later? Can you drink the free coffee at work, or are you willing to tell your eighteen-year-old child that she "can't go to college because back when you were little Mommy and Daddy simply couldn't get through the morning without a custom-made double espresso."

Making Your Child Wealthy and Wise

Despite all the good things we get during the accumulation phase of investing for our children, the great, glorious prize comes at the end of the journey. I have a client who, through hard work and disciplined investing, was able to buy a new house for his daughter. I still remember how proud he was when the sale was completed. I don't think I've seen a bigger smile on someone *receiving* a six-figure sum of money, much less a person writing a check for that amount.

But securing your child's financial future might actually give you a new worry. And it involves the murky, undefined area that all parents deal with: Am I giving my child just enough to survive and thrive, or is it too much? How do you start investing for your child, grow your small savings into a larger amount for her, and then give her the money without making her spoiled and lazy?

Don't worry.

Money won't build or destroy your child's character. Money will reveal it.

I have been closely involved with thousands of people from hundreds of families, from all walks of life and all levels of wealth. In my experience a lot more people have been helped by having the seeds of financial independence planted by their parents than have been hurt by it.

Why might this be hard to believe? Because well-balanced, independently wealthy people who continue to live in moderation look just like everybody *else!* These are the "millionaires next door" we've heard about. They drive sensible cars, live in comfortable, practical homes, and even continue to work at jobs they find rewarding. Their identities and self-worth have nothing to do with their money, so they don't feel the need to wave their wealth in our faces at every opportunity.

Some of the nicest people I know are wealthy, and I've met

some insufferable egomaniacs who are dirt poor. You could transpose the bank accounts from one group to the other, and I bet everybody would still act the same as always. For better or worse, money isn't going to change who our children are or how they behave.

There is a natural arc to the process of investing for your child. There is usually little or no money at the beginning, yet with disciplined saving and investing, the sum begins to grow. Eventually the "accumulation" phase ends, the value of the investments peaks, and the "distribution" phase begins. And the key to raising a well-adjusted *and* financially secure child lies in gradually growing her knowledge while you grow her assets, and then progressively releasing more money as she matures.

You can certainly accumulate money for your kid without her knowing about it. But by slowly bringing your child into the mix, you can teach her and help her make decisions.

It's never too early to start investing for your child, and it's never too early to start teaching her, either. Ever since I was able to get Ellie to stop putting coins in her mouth, we have gone through a saving ritual when I get home from work. Before I change into my "play" clothes, I give all my spare change to her. She cups her tiny little hands around the coins, dutifully carries them over to a five-gallon jug in the corner of the room, and drops them in with the rest of the previous deposits. She's at the point now where when we are on a walk and she finds a coin on the sidewalk, she turns to me excitedly and says, "Put in jar?" and then carries the dime or nickel all the way home.

Now, I could probably get that change in the jug a lot faster on my own. But by involving Ellie, I have shown her how her actions can help the pile of money grow, and now she buys into the idea of saving and accumulating.

Once you have decided to relinquish control of the money to your child, you can help her keep her financial balance by starting small, and making the amounts larger as she grows older. It is much better to allow her to "grow into" her money, rather than just surprising her with a gigantic check, bellowing, "Congratulations!" like some Ed McMahon impersonator.

Think of providing financial security for your child in the same way you would teach her to ride a bicycle. You would never prop a toddler on the seat of a mountain bike and let go. When she is ready, you purchase a small bicycle equipped with training wheels. You explain to her how the pedals work, how to steer with the handlebars, and how to apply the brakes. You teach her to go slowly, watch for cars, and obey the traffic laws. Eventually you take the training wheels off, and you run behind her as she pedals, holding the seat to keep her steady. Soon you release your grip on the bike. She may ride a few yards before she falls over, and she'll probably get a few scrapes and scratches in the process. But after a while, she can ride farther and farther without falling, and, in time, she gets the hang of it. She is ecstatic, and I'm guessing you are pretty proud, too.

Depositing funds in an investment account is like buying the bicycle. It doesn't do much good to just give your child the bike without teaching her to ride, and it won't help to use the financial strategies in this book without teaching her the principles and standards needed to manage money responsibly.

I would even argue that instruction along the "arc" is at least as important as investment when it comes to raising a financially secure child. But just by virtue of being her parent, you are already demonstrating the values she will need to manage her money effectively. If you need a little help, turn ahead to the section "Ten Things You Need to Know" (see page 35).

You Can Do It!

Whether you have saved any money for her yet or not, you are already "investing" in your child: your love, your time, and your energy. Just by becoming a parent, you've committed to putting a lot of money toward your child's future. It costs anywhere from $150,000 to $300,000 to raise a child to age eighteen, according to a U.S. Department of Agriculture study.

Dr. Benjamin Spock's best advice to parents was to "trust yourselves." And those words of wisdom also apply to securing your child's financial future. Don't be paralyzed by the fear of picking the wrong investment vehicle. Doing something is much better than doing nothing.

And not only is investing for your child much less stressful than "not investing," it can also be more enjoyable than investing for yourself. It doesn't matter if the stock market crashes the day after you open an account for your child. Depending on the goal, your kid has a horizon from several years to several decades in the future, so the pressure is off. Putting money aside for your kid isn't about what Greenspan, Microsoft, or some foreign dictator is going to do. It's about what *you* are going to do.

But the clock is ticking. The longer you delay taking action, the harder it will be for your child to become financially independent. A dollar a day saved at 10% annually gives a newborn baby over $2.4 million at age sixty-five, but waiting until the child turns five will give her almost a million dollars less at retirement.

Still, if your child *is* five, and you haven't done anything, don't worry—you can still reach $2.4 million when your child turns sixty-five by upping the daily deposit to just $1.63!

In thirteen years as an investment adviser, and talking to thousands of people about their money and their lives, I have never heard anyone say these two things:

"I'm glad we didn't invest any money for our kids!"

and

"I'm glad my parents didn't invest any money for me!"

You knew that making your child financially independent was the right thing to do even before you picked up this book. You just needed to know how to do it. Combined with lots of love and a little money, the information in this book will give you everything you need to get tax savings and peace of mind now, and to provide your child with a secure and enjoyable life later.

Ten Things You Need to Know

If You're Going to Make Your Kid a Millionaire

Secure—Easy in mind; confident; free from danger, risk, loss, or deprivation.

Insecure—Not highly stable or well adjusted; not firmly fastened or fixed; beset by fear and anxiety.

—*Merriam-Webster's Collegiate Dictionary*

Like lawyers, psychologists, and members of the clergy, financial advisers get a behind-the-scenes look at how people's lives really are. As a firsthand witness to the triumphs, tragedy, and tedium families experience, I have seen how human nature impacts their relationship to money. Two words describe the contrast between the financial status and general existence of those who are financially independent and those who struggle: secure and insecure.

The "Secures" have a certain calm about their investment matters, and their lives in general.

They care enough to make sure their portfolios are in good shape, but they don't get too excited about day-to-day movements in the stock market.

They have good relationships with their spouses and families.

They measure life over decades, rather than weeks.

They work hard at jobs they like, but still have a healthy balance between working and playing.

They drive reasonable, reliable cars, and live in well-kept homes.

They usually are debt-free, and if they do have outstanding loans, the principal was used only to help grow their business (and their financial independence).

They like quality over quantity.

They have a concern for their community and their future generations.

• • •

"Insecures," however, ride a roller coaster of financial chaos.

They believe there is a direct correlation between their net worth and their happiness.

They may make a decent living, but they spend as much as—or more than—they earn.

They view long-term as six months, and are constantly searching to make a quick buck.

They are in debt because of purchases that have no possible return of investment.

They equate money with love and purchase things they believe will enhance their status with others.

Their financial turmoil takes a toll on their family and friendships.

They generally dislike their jobs.

In short, they have a gaping emotional "hole" they are trying to fill with money. And the harder they try to become "rich," the bigger the hole gets.

• • •

I first thought the Secures were secure because they were wealthy, and the Insecures were unhappy because they had little or no net worth. But as I paid closer attention to these two groups, I learned that the amount of money a person has has nothing to do with how fulfilled he is.

The booming stock market of the 1990s couldn't help but make some of the Insecures wealthy beyond even their expectations. As these people became rich, I thought they would have a change in attitude and start behaving more like Secures. I thought the Insecures would feel as if they had "made it." They could relax, stop worrying about money, and address some of the other issues in their lives.

I couldn't have been more wrong. The new prosperity caused a giddy delight in some of the Insecures. But as the thrill of the new dollars wore off, I think these people realized one thing: it wasn't enough. Not "enough" as in "enough to live on," but rather "enough to make them happy." They spent more, invested more recklessly, and began agonizing over the wild swings in the market. I adopted the role of moderator in their lives, rather than adviser. My main job consisted of trying to smooth their highs and lows. I tried to prevent them from first getting too "irrationally exuberant" (to paraphrase the immortal words of Alan Greenspan), and then to keep them from abandoning all the long-term plans we had created.

In contrast, the bull market of the 1990s hardly changed the attitude of the Secures. Don't get me wrong—they liked making money! But they realized what can go up can also go down, and they didn't make any rash moves based on the great rises and rapid falls we went through. They didn't change their lifestyles dramatically, didn't quit their jobs just because they could, and didn't start buying $17,000 gas grills to replace the Weber they bought at Wal-Mart.

Most of us are somewhere in between these two groups. But which type of person do you want to emulate? Me, too! Luckily for both of us, during my career I learned a lot from being an intimate part of the lives of Secures and Insecures. Both groups have taught me valuable lessons that I can apply to my own life, and also pass on to "in betweens."

I have compiled the following list as a guide to help you, and to give you some things you may wish to impart to your children. Following these ten guidelines will not guarantee your child will become a millionaire, just as ignoring them won't ensure a lifetime of poverty for him. But I believe you can dramatically increase your child's chances of becoming a Secure by learning these fundamentals for yourself, and teaching them to him.

1. Time Is Your Best Friend Depending on the age of your child and the goal you're shooting for, you could have anywhere from a few years to half a century to save and invest. And the more time you have, the less money you need to invest. As a matter of fact, if you have a newborn baby, you can put aside as little as $13 per month (about 41 cents per day) and still make your child a millionaire at age sixty-five!

	Monthly savings required to make a kid a millionaire (Assuming a 10% annual return)
Time frame (in years)	Amount
65	$ 13
60	22
55	35
50	58
45	96
40	158
35	264
30	442
25	753
20	1,317
15	2,412

As your time frame shrinks, the amount of the required monthly deposit skyrockets!

A long time frame not only reduces the amount of money you need to save, it also increases the likelihood that your investment will pay off, and makes it less likely that you and your child will be affected by short-term swings in the value of his investment portfolio. With history as a guide, in any given year there is about a one in three chance that the value of the Standard & Poor's 500 index will end lower than it started. But that probability drops to less than one in twenty over any ten-year period. And by starting early, you can accumulate greater amounts of money to protect your child in the event of the inevitable market downturn.

2. Procrastination Is Your Worst Enemy The longer you wait to start, the more money you need to save. And the closer you are to your goal, the more likely it is that you and your child will be affected by a plummeting market. You may think this is redundant after reading "Ten Things You Need To Know," #1. But it is so important that you do something—anything—today that I want to drill it into your head.

I have set up hundreds of accounts for the benefit of children. With almost every one, I heard a common refrain from the parent, grandparent, or loving relative initiating the transaction: "I just wish I had started this sooner."

After hearing this a few times, I began asking, "Why didn't you?" The replies I got were along four different lines, and in case you would have similar answers, I have included my reason why you can't use them as excuses!

Answer	My response
"I didn't think I had enough money."	You can start an account with as little as $25.
"I wasn't sure how to go about it."	Mark Twain said, "We're all ignorant, just about different things." This book gives you all you need to get started.

Answer	**My response**
"I was afraid of doing the wrong thing."	Doing nothing is a much bigger mistake than doing the wrong thing.
"I just finally got around to it."	That's easy to understand. And after you spend a few hours and a few dollars, you can get back to the rest of your life.

One immutable law of physics is that children grow faster than we can keep up with. I've never heard anyone say to a child, "What, you're still only ten? I thought you'd be about fourteen by now." The few hours it takes to begin investing for a child today can spare you a lifetime of regret.

3. Without a Foundation, the Structure Crumbles You can provide all the financial assets in the world for a child, but unless you equip him with the tools to be emotionally stable and financially responsible, the money is not going to help. In fact, it may even lead to more problems.

Think back to the contrast between the Secures and the Insecures. I have a hunch I could take all the assets from the Secures and give them to the Insecures. Within a decade, I would be willing to bet that the Secure group would once again be financially independent, while the Insecures would be back to near poverty.

Your investing now is an indelible demonstration of your values. Kids see and hear everything, and through your own examples, you can help ensure that your child will avoid throwing away the money you have provided for him. He might impart these same lessons to his children, along with providing the assets to secure their financial independence. Your actions today could affect your future generations for hundreds of years.

4. Watched Pots Never Boil, and Watched Stocks Never Double Investing is one of the few endeavors where constant monitoring of the subject can actually reduce your effectiveness. You don't need to know every single intimate detail about every single one of your investments all the time to make money.

It's kind of like boarding an airplane. You would never think to ask the gate attendant if you could just spend a couple hours looking over the engines, examining the landing gear, and interrogating the pilot and his crew. And if you ever stopped to think about all the millions of things that need to go right for your flight to be successful, you would turn and run back down the concourse, looking for a skycap to drive you to your destination in his little luggage cart.

When I first began investing I was convinced that the reason I lost money was that I didn't have enough information. I tried to keep up with every market fluctuation, earnings report, and change in research coverage. It took me a few months of chasing my own tail to realize that someone would always have better information and would always get it quicker.

Looking for guidance, I decided to pay attention to the way my Secure clients dealt with the avalanche of information, the volatile swings in the market, and the speed-of-light pace at which things changed in the investment world.

Not only did I find a common denominator in the way these people made money over the long term, but I also found a few components to their strategy that might be of interest to the average investor:

- They pay little or no taxes on their investments
- They spend almost nothing in commissions and fees

- They put very little time into monitoring their portfolio

It sounds pretty good, doesn't it? Here is the secret investment strategy of secure investors:

They Put Their Money in Sensible Investments and Then They Get On with Their Lives!

Isn't that disappointing? Don't you wish I'd said, "Buy when the thirty-year Treasury yield reaches pi times the S&P 500 dividend yield, sell when Alan Greenspan gets a fever, unless it's the Tuesday before triple-witching"? I wish it were that complicated, because my knowledge would be that much more valuable.

Over the long term (I'm talking *decades*), the best-performing investors I've seen don't buy and sell. They hold. They don't follow their stocks daily—at the most they might check the value of the portfolio each quarter. They don't watch the cable TV investment channels or worry if the Fed raises or lowers rates. And because they rarely sell, they pay very little in taxes or trading costs.

Whether they are consciously aware of their behavior or not, these people are on to something. The reason too much information can be dangerous to a long-term investor is that making money in investments is not so much about intelligence as it is about emotion and discipline. Investors who follow the day-to-day movements of the market tend to get swayed by the smallest of downturns, and they react accordingly.

They feel that if they could just get in on the "up" days and out on the "down" days, they would be successful beyond their wildest dreams. They try to guess when these days are going to be, an exercise that is not much different from guessing "heads" or "tails" when flipping a coin. As they begin to make a few mistakes, the anxiety of the Insecures takes over and whips them into a trading frenzy. Eventually they are wiped out financially or emotionally, or both.

The logic behind the "no attention" investment strategy has been further proven outside the stock market. What investment did post–World War II middle-class Americans use (more than all other investments) to accumulate wealth? Their house, of course. Even today, many of us have a large amount of our net worth tied up in our homes. And if you've owned a house over the last five or six years, chances are you've seen its value increase dramatically.

Think of your investments in the same way that you think about owning a home. One reason people are able to accumulate wealth via their home is that they don't get scared into selling the house just because prices are falling. If you're not moving, you're not going to sell your house. And if you're not going to sell your house, you don't really care what the day-to-day value is.

As a matter of fact, the only way you can truly know what the daily cash value of your home is, is to call a real estate agent every day and tell her, "It's me again. I want to know what the highest price is you can get me today for my house. I'll call you in few hours to see what kinds of bids you get." Most of the time, you probably wouldn't be too happy with the prices she brought back to you. Daily fluctuations of 20% would not be uncommon, and eventually the agent would file a temporary restraining order against you.

It sounds ludicrous to do this with your house, but this is exactly what Insecures do with their investment portfolios. All of the information, access, and liquidity available becomes a curse, rather than a blessing, to Insecure investors. They call the toll-free number provided by their 401(k) administrator each day, or download their closing stock and mutual fund prices the minute they are available on the Internet. Then they either celebrate how much they've "made," or bemoan the huge "loss" they've suffered. They vow to make some changes the next day to get into what's "hot" or what's "moving," but pretty soon, they've transacted themselves into the ground. Only by giving up can they get back on the road to prosperity.

5. Wealth Equals Freedom Not status, not power, not intelligence. How rich do you have to be, to be "rich"? My definition is that you have enough money to support your desired lifestyle. And that's it. After that, it's all relative. You could have a $10 million net worth and be pitied by people in the Hamptons, yet a thousand dollars is a year's income for millions of people in the world.

6. We Are Who We Are, Not What We Have "He buys things he doesn't need, with money he doesn't have, to impress people he doesn't like." How many of us know people fitting that description? When I was younger, I fell prey to judging people by their possessions, rather than their character. Nice Mercedes, big house, huge boat, stunning lake home—must be a great guy. Make no mistake, I did meet plenty of people who had some or all of these things, and today I still respect them. But I also met some jerks to whom I realize I gave more praise than they deserved, just because they made some impressive purchases. I was especially disappointed to find out how many of these "big spenders" bought these items on credit! And, regrettably, I dismissed some wonderful people who happened to live in nondescript houses and drove a small car with 120,000 miles and a few rust spots.

Now, however, I tend to have a little more respect for those people who are living below their means. And I try to concentrate on a person's good deeds (rather than their goods), especially when my daughter is in earshot.

7. Money Is a Tool, Not a Weapon If your child asked you to help him build a tree house, you would probably pick up your hammer at the first opportunity and get to work. But you would never dream of using the hammer in a threatening manner to make your child do what you want. Yet that is what many parents do with their money when they use it as a reward, or use withholding it as a threat. It sometimes seems like an easy out to appeal to a kid's material wants and needs to make him behave in a certain way, but it sets up a dangerous association in his mind that can cause both of you great harm down the road.

Does that mean you just have to give up control of any money you've accumulated for your child, regardless of how he intends to use and abuse it? Of course not. But you can lay down some basic standards as to what you feel is acceptable, and then give your child the opportunity to demonstrate what he has learned from you. Understand that, as with most everything involving children, he is going to do few things that you don't agree with. But he will probably use most of your financial benevolence in ways that are agreeable to you. If so, you can gradually release more money as he grows older.

8. The Second-Greatest Gift The first and greatest gift you can give any child is your love. After that, the next-greatest thing (despite what the good people at Toys "R" Us say) is financial independence. I'm not saying you need to ignore a kid's wishes for Tickle Me Elmo, but sometimes we go a little overboard.

In the first year after my daughter was born, I would guess she received over $3,000 worth of toys, outfits, and books from friends and family. All were purchased new, and we were very thankful for the thoughtfulness behind each one. But you can guess what my daughter thought of those gifts. She would rather play with the wrapping paper and cardboard than just about anything. And she sure didn't notice if these presents were bought for $30 retail, or 50 cents at a garage sale.

Now part of exchanging gifts is that the giver gets to choose whatever she wants to express her love for the recipient. But if you have a child whom you would like to become financially independent, think about how powerful a $50 deposit today into a growth mutual fund would be after fifty years. At 10%, it would be over $5,800! How does that compare to the enjoyment a six-month-old is going to receive from that particular toy or doll?

9. It's Easier to Spend Less Than It Is to Make More There are millions more people who have achieved financial independence by spending less than they earned than all the lottery winners, day traders, and Internet entrepreneurs combined. Look at it this way: for every dollar you can avoid spending right now, you will have $117 in fifty years, if compounded annually at 10%. Think about that when you are deciding to trade in your paid-up car for a new one (and a new payment schedule). Fifty years from now, what do you think your child will wish you had done?

10. People Get Rich Slowly I know: the problem with instant gratification is that it takes too long. But people trying to get rich quickly usually find they get *poor* even faster. Who didn't take just a wee bit of perverse pleasure in the obliteration of the dot-com millionaires in 2000? (I wish they'd put as many of these people on magazine covers for *losing* the money as they did for making it.) This boom and bust confirmed what we already knew to be true. Somehow I don't think the phrase "easy come, easy go" has been around this long without having a lot of truth to it.

A Few Things That Will Help You Use This Book Effectively

1. What Can You Do *Now*? In this book I humbly offer up what might be an overwhelming array of choices and options to make your child financially independent. At the end of each chapter (where appropriate) I list the advantages and disadvantages of each method so you can weigh each idea against the others. Hopefully, one or two will jump out at you as being the best solution for you and your family.

However, I also realize that you might not have the time to fully investigate each method. Yet you still need to make an intelligent and informed decision about where to devote your dollars. The following lists reflect what I feel are the most urgent needs, and where the most powerful opportunities lie, for a family with small children:

Must do

1. Wills, guardians, and life insurance (Chapter 3)
2. Save for college (Chapter 2)
3. Systematic deposits into a mutual fund (Chapter 1)
4. Deposit into your Roth IRA (Chapter 5)

Biggest bang for the buck

1. Save for college (Chapter 2)
2. Your kid's Roth IRA (Chapter 8)
3. Deposit into a variable annuity (Chapter 4)
4. Grandparents help (Chapter 13)
5. Your Roth IRA (Chapter 5)
6. Start your kid early in his 401(k) (Chapter 9)

Of course, you should devote the bulk of your attention to
the goals that are right around the corner (like college) and put
more of your money toward the needs that are going to cost the
most. This is especially true if you already have children, and
reading this book represents the first move you have made to
provide for their future.

If this describes you, don't beat yourself up over your procrastination; instead, celebrate finally taking action that might
do wonders for your child. Keep repeating this to yourself:
"Late is *so* much better than *never!*"

**2. After "Now," Go Back to the Past, and Then On to the Fu-
ture** I am a sucker for those charts and tables in parenting mag-
azines and books showing "Where Your Child Should Be" in
her growth or development. I eagerly turn right to Ellie's age
and rejoice if she is a little "ahead" of the norm, and if she is behind the average I start looking for a specialist in the Yellow
Pages.

But I usually ignore the information given for kids younger
than Ellie, and I don't pay much attention to the numbers for
the older children. So I sure can't blame you if you notice that I
organized the book according to the ideal moves at every stage
of a child's life, and then quickly turn to the pages that discuss
what to do at your kid's current age (you've probably already
done that—if not, go ahead. I'll wait).

But after you check what you should be doing for your kids
today, don't just toss the book aside and dash out the door to
the corner brokerage. First, go over any chapters covering your
child's earlier years (along with the "Must Do" list above) to
make sure you haven't missed any important moves. Also,
read ahead so you have a preview of what you can do in the
coming years (they'll be here before you know it). You might
even learn a few things about your *own* investments; if so,
there's no extra charge for that.

3. The 10% Solution Whenever I am making a hypothetical
projection of what the long-term rate of return might be on dol-

lars invested in a growth-oriented account, I use an annual rate of 10%. This number (like the other ones I use in projections) is for illustrative purposes only. Your actual rate of return is likely to be anything *but* 10% depending on a few factors:

- *The types of investments you choose*   Stocks generally provide greater long-term return and short-term volatility than bonds. Bonds usually provide greater long-term return and short-term volatility than cash money market accounts. And cash money market accounts *always* provide greater return than burying money in your backyard.
- *Your child's investment time frame*   The longer you have to invest for him, the more likely the "return ranking" of stocks, bonds, and cash above is to come true.
- *The actions of you and your child during good and bad times*   All investments go through periods of popularity and contempt. If you and your child put money in at the highs, and then take it out at the lows, you are likely to end up with hardly anything at all.
- *What the future holds*   No one knows what stocks will do in the future. The historic average annual returns for stocks (with dividends reinvested) is roughly between 9% and 11%, depending on whom you ask and how they came up with their numbers. And even the value of *these* figures is questionable; as any investor will read again and again, "Past performance is no indication of future results."

4. The Only Thing That Stays the Same Is the Fact That Things Change The basic philosophy of this book has been true for thousands of years: we all want the lives of our children to be better than ours. But the devil is in the details, and no more so than when investing for your child. The abundance of information I've provided means that some of it might be dated by the time it gets to you. Companies merge, Web sites close down, tax rates and laws change, investment "windows of opportunity" open and close, and a financial strategy that may seem ludicrous for your family today could become a magic carpet ride to prosperity only a few years from now.

These truths don't give you an excuse to throw up your hands and do nothing. Instead, they only point out that although I've listed the best routes to your child's financial independence, you might encounter a few roadblocks on the way. So you need to stay alert to find the detours that will still lead to your destination.

I hope you and your family enjoy the ride.

PART ONE
Prebirth to Six Years

This section will give you everything you need to cover the basic necessities of providing for a child. All three chapters in this part cover subjects that can be addressed and started for under a few hundred dollars.

That's probably a relief to you, because money might be a little tight for you during these years. You may have just purchased a house or quit your job to stay home with your child until he goes to kindergarten. And the cost of diapers, formula, and child care are new additions to your monthly budget.

The last chapter in this section deals with a subject that no one wants to address, yet everyone must: What would happen to your child if you and your spouse weren't around to care for him? Relax. The chances of your dying before your child can care for himself are tiny. But we all know of a family devastated by the unexpected death of one (or both) parents. Most parents won't leave enough money to properly care for their children, and the majority don't even have a will.

If you fall into either category, don't feel bad. I don't blame you for putting off the subject of your own death. But take a few minutes to read the chapter, and then get started on a proper will and obtaining enough life insurance. It won't take more than a few hours of your time over a week or two, and you'll be surprised by how inexpensive the whole process is. The peace of mind you'll have afterward, though, is priceless.

chapter one

Put in Thirty Minutes Now and $1 Every Day and Have a Millionaire Kid Later

Turning Tiny Dollars into Big Ones

Imagine that through some strange twist of fate (either that, or you're stuck in a doctor's waiting room), you actually have time to look at a magazine. You read an article containing an interview with a top investment manager. She has an impressive track record and is paid millions of dollars per year in salary and bonuses. In the interview she expresses her economic philosophy in a way that makes sense to you. You decide you would like her to invest your money for your child.

You call her office, are lucky enough to get through to speak with her, and you tell her something like this: "Hello, I'm trying to make my kid a millionaire, and I'd like you to help me. I'm going to send you $500 initially on behalf of my child, and I would like you to withdraw $50 per month from my checking account and invest that, too. Spread that money among your hundred or so favorite stocks, and keep an eye on those stocks so you can buy and sell when you think it's appropriate. I need you to provide the daily value of my account to me, and I would like the opportunity to take the money out whenever I feel like it. In return, I will pay you a few dollars a year for this service. How about it? . . . Hello?"

The request *seems* ludicrous. But what you asked for is exactly what is available in almost every mutual fund.

Using a mutual fund is the easiest and most basic way to begin securing your financial goals for your child. According to the Investment Company Institute, over 35 million Americans are using this method to accumulate anywhere from a few hundred to a few million dollars for the benefit of a child. It has the lowest initial minimums, the greatest flexibility, and the widest range of choices of any investment option you have. As a matter of fact, if you have $50 you can spare, you can read this chapter in a few minutes, take the action steps at the end, and be well on your way to building your child's financial independence.

What Is a Mutual Fund?

Don't beat yourself up if you don't know. Despite the fact that the majority of American households contain a mutual fund owner, none of these people was born with an innate knowledge of financial vehicles, either.

A group of investors' money is put together in a mutual fund to purchase and sell an assortment of investments. There are mutual funds that buy stocks, bonds, and real estate properties and loan payment pools. Some funds buy a combination of these types of securities. Other funds may confine their investments to a single country or a single industry. Like most investors, you will probably be best served by the most prevalent type of fund structure, known as the "open-end" mutual fund. That's the type I'll talk about in this chapter.

The fund is usually managed by an individual or a team of individuals hired by the mutual fund company (unless it is an index fund—see page 60). These people buy and sell stocks and bonds according to certain criteria including:

- The fund's goals and objectives
- The manager's economic forecast
- The amount of cash on hand, determined by investors making deposits and withdrawals from the fund

A fund will state its investment philosophy in its prospectus, a legal document that the mutual fund company is required to furnish to all prospective investors. You can receive the prospectus via regular mail, or download it from the mutual fund company's Web site. The prospectus also tells about the fund's past performance, expenses, and sales charges, and any other disclosures that are required by law to be made to potential investors.

Everybody will tell you to review the prospectus carefully before you invest, and you should. But it is written in such dense "legalese" that you might not believe even the people who wrote the prospectus have read it. Try to get through it as best you can, but don't let the complexity intimidate you into avoiding the mutual fund.

Which Mutual Fund Should You Use?

This is one of the most perplexing questions mutual fund investors face. Part of the problem stems from the fact that there are over ten thousand mutual funds available to the general public. And the confusion is compounded by magazine covers that scream headlines like "FOUR FUNDS YOU MUST OWN NOW TO AVOID SPONTANEOUS COMBUSTION!!!"

The disappointing news for you is that you can do all the homework in the world, study every single one of the thousands of mutual funds out there, and you still won't know which one is most likely to make your kid a millionaire. And I could give you the ten funds I think will make the most money over the next twelve months. But even if I were right (I wouldn't be), by the time you read this the year would be just about over.

That said, there are some ways you can quickly winnow the thousands of funds down to ones that make the most sense for you and your child.

1. Past Performance Is No Guarantee of Future Results These words (or some like it) are contained in the ads and prospectus of almost every mutual fund. And they are there for good reason.

When you start to investigate mutual funds, you're going to be tempted to invest in the fund that is up the most so far in the last year/quarter/fifteen minutes. These guys must know something, right?

Wrong. Most mutual fund managers do not have the freedom to buy whatever they want. Instead, the fund managers have to invest within a certain area, like growth stocks, value stocks, big companies, small companies, tech stocks, health care stocks, government bonds—whatever fits within the parameters established by the fund company.

Eventually, the types of investments the fund holds become popular (it's proof of the truth of the phrase "every dog has his day"). Money starts chasing this particular sector, boosting the prices of the securities in the mutual fund. As the prices rise, the value of shareholders' accounts rises.

This is great if you were in the fund before the holdings became desirable; you probably made a lot of money.

But if you put your money into a mutual fund that has outperformed recently, you are buying a type of investment that has already gone through a "boom." The better it has done and the more it has gone up, the closer you are to the "bust," and the less likely there is any profit left for you in the near term.

Picking a fund based on past performance is like moving according to what the weather is like *right now.* If you are living in the northeastern United States in January, Phoenix looks like a great place to be. You pack up the family, buy a house, and pretty soon you're basking in the dry desert heat. But within a few months, summer rolls around. That "dry heat" starts to feel like a blast furnace, and you'll be longing for the moderate warmth of your former home.

Or look at it like this: investing your child's money according to recent performance is like hopping on a roller coaster in the middle of the ride. If you get on after it has made a long, uninterrupted climb, you might be in for a rapid fall (if you doubt me on this, ask anyone who bought a fund focused on Internet stocks in March 2000).

Don't worry. The bad news is that you are not going to pick the "best" mutual fund out there. The good news is that all you need to do is pick a fund that does pretty well, and pretty well should be good enough.

2. What I Look For Your needs might be the exact opposite of mine. Or they could be identical, and you might invest in a mutual fund that meets my requirements, only to see the value of your account go down and stay down. That said, I've found beginning mutual fund investors tend to feel more comfortable with a fund if it has:

- A long history of operation
- Continuity of management
- Recognizable, "blue-chip" companies in the portfolio

I also think novices fare best with "Goldilocks" types of funds (not too hot, and not too cold). These accounts usually don't make as much money as other funds in good times, but they don't lose as much in bad times.

3. Minimize Expenses Although expenses and fees definitely matter, your success as a mutual fund investor has little to do with whether you pay a commission. There are plenty of great funds that are sold through advisers and have a sales charge, and there are lots of wonderful no-load (meaning no sales charge) funds that you can purchase on your own. Like yard-work, home improvements, and oil changes, the issue is whether you're willing and able to do the work yourself, or if you would rather pay someone to do it for you.

Even if you pick a no-load fund on your own, it will still cost you. There are expenses to running a mutual fund, like salaries, trading costs, and accounting services. And, like any other business, the mutual fund company wants to make a profit. So the fund will pass on its costs to all of the shareholders via something called the expense ratio—the cost of running the fund, divided by the assets in the fund. The expense ratio can range from nothing (if the fund company is temporarily eating the fund's operating expenses) up to several percentage points. The average expense ratio for a stock fund is around 1.5% per year.

A fund may also charge a marketing and distribution fee (called a "12b-1" expense) that can be as high as 1% of assets each year. But many funds don't levy this fee, and those that do usually ding shareholders for about ½% or less.

These costs are disclosed in most complete fund reports, including the prospectus. You don't pay these fees separately. Instead, the expenses are deducted from the gross return of the fund. If your money in the fund grew at a 10% rate in one year, and the annual expenses equaled 1.5%, you would have netted only 8.5%.

A fund with higher costs must give you better performance, right? Not necessarily. As a matter of fact, there is very little data saying you get what you pay for when it comes to mutual fund annual expenses. And all other things being equal, a fund with lower annual expenses will outperform one with higher costs.

This is especially important over the many years during your child's investment horizon. If, for example, you are investing $50 per month for sixty years, and Fund X has ½% higher annual expenses than the otherwise equal Fund Y, you would have a much greater amount in the cheaper fund (assuming a 10% net annual return in the more cost-efficient fund):

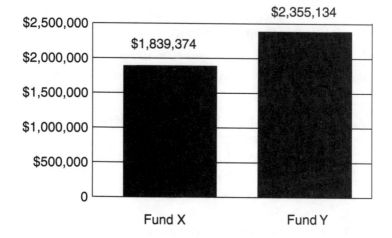

Expenses Add Up

Half a percent annually could mean a half-million dollars!

4. Minimize Taxes Net income and capital gains earned by a mutual fund must be distributed each year to the shareholders, who pay taxes on them. But mutual funds that seldom sell securities generally generate fewer capital gains, and therefore less tax liability to their shareholders. This is especially important if you are going to:

1. Keep the fund in your name (and your tax bracket) or
2. Keep it in your under-fourteen-year-old child's name, but through either your deposits or growth of the fund, eventually accumulate enough so that any net distributions might exceed the tax-advantaged amounts (in 2002

the first $750 is tax-free, the next $750 is taxed
at your child's rate—everything else is taxed
at your highest rate). It's hard to say what size
account may generate over $1,500 in annual
distributions, but it's more likely on anything
over $10,000. If you think you will have this
amount in the account well before your child
turns fourteen, you should pay special attention
to the tax liability of a fund.

What can you do to avoid a potentially painful distribution?

1. Look for funds with low tax liabilities and
    portfolio turnover.
2. If securing a comfortable retirement for your
    child is your main goal, consider putting the
    money in a tax-sheltered variable annuity
    (see Chapter 4).
3. Choose a tax-advantaged mutual fund (see
    the Eaton Vance example in "Just for Kids,"
    opposite). Although relatively new, these
    funds are purportedly managed so that
    relatively few net gains are realized, thereby
    minimizing the tax liability.

5. Index Funds One type of fund that usually has lower expense ratios and lower ongoing tax liability is called an index
fund. Index funds are unmanaged—but don't worry, that
doesn't mean that your money sits in a pile on the office floor
until somebody gets around to investing it.

Instead, these funds invest your money in a ratio equal to
the makeup of a particular index. When companies are added
or subtracted to the index (a usually infrequent occurrence), the
fund company sells the stocks taken out and buys the ones
added in. Index funds are most popular with investors who be-

lieve active management hurts long-term performance, rather than helps it.

There are several funds that mimic many different indexes, but the most popular index tracked is the Standard & Poor's 500. And the largest single S&P 500 index fund is the Vanguard 500 Index fund (www.vanguard.com). It is also one of the most popular funds in existence, with millions of shareholders and tens of billions of dollars in assets.

6. The Bigger the Better? Not necessarily. But if you believe there is strength in numbers, you may be comforted in knowing that millions of other people are investing in the same fund as you, and are sharing your pains and your gains. Of all the funds that invest in stocks (or stocks and bonds), these had the largest assets as of February 28, 2001, according to the Investment Company Institute:

Fund

1. Fidelity Magellan
2. Vanguard 500 Index
3. American Funds: Investment Company of America
4. American Funds: Washington Mutual Fund
5. Fidelity Growth and Income
6. Fidelity Contrafund
7. American Funds: Growth Fund
8. Janus Fund
9. American Funds: EuroPacific
10. American Funds: New Perspective

7. Just for Kids There are several funds that have been developed with an eye toward kids, and the people who invest for kids. These funds may not do any better (or worse) than normal mutual funds. But most of the funds buy companies that children may appreciate, like Disney or McDonald's. And these (and many other financial service companies) have marketing and fund information designed for children, which may help spur your child's interest in investing.

Fund Name	Phone Number	Web Site
Stein Roe Young Investor	1-800-338-2550	www.younginvestor.com
USAA First Start Growth	1-800-292-8302	www.usaa.com
Eaton Vance Tax-Managed Young Shareholder	1-800-262-1122	www.eatonvance.com
Royce Trust & GiftShares	1-800-221-4268	www.roycefunds.com

Putting Money in the Fund

1. Your Initial Deposit Almost all mutual funds require an initial deposit ranging from $25 to $100,000, depending on which fund you use. Several hundred companies offer mutual funds that have minimum initial deposits of only $250, and if you have at least $1,000, you can choose from thousands of mutual funds.

2. Future Contributions You can also contribute more to the account in the future whenever you like, with a minimum subsequent deposit that can be $50 or less. But one of the smartest ways to accumulate money in a mutual fund is called "dollar-cost averaging." Dollar-cost averaging involves depositing the same dollar amount into a mutual fund at regular intervals over a period of time.

For instance, you may put a $500 initial deposit into a mutual fund, and then instruct the fund to withdraw $50 per month from your checking account and deposit it into the mutual fund. The fund company will do this for you at no extra cost, beyond any applicable sales charges. You can raise or lower the dollar amount at any time. You can halt the payments and then begin them again. You can even make sporadic deposits into the fund along with the systematic deposits. The only stipulation the mutual fund company may make is that each deposit must be at least a certain amount, usually $25. If you can't afford to put $25 per month into the account, you can contribute quarterly, semiannually, or even annually.

Monitoring Your Fund

1. Calculating Your Account Value Regardless of whether you use the assistance of an adviser or choose your fund yourself, you will want to know how to figure out how much your fund account is worth (only periodically—see "Ten Things You Need to Know," #4, page 41).

The open-end mutual fund is priced by adding up the total value of the assets in the fund, and dividing that amount by the number of shares outstanding. If the fund is priced at $10 per share and you invest $1,000, you would own a hundred shares of the mutual fund. The price is calculated at the close of each trading day. The number of shares you have is constant (unless you buy more shares or have your dividends reinvested), but the dollar value per share will fluctuate according to the value of the assets.

2. Capital Gains and Income The fund is required by law to distribute all net income and capital gains to shareholders each year. This can happen quarterly, or one or two times late in the year, or not at all. You can take these distributions in the form of cash, but almost all funds allow you to direct the fund to automatically reinvest the payouts into more shares of the fund, and at no additional cost.

Even if you choose to have these distributions reinvested into more shares of the fund, unless the fund is held in an IRA or similar tax-deferred account, the distributions are taxable.

Advantages of a Mutual Fund

1. Low Initial Deposit This method allows you to start investing for your child for less than the cost of your weekly grocery bill. Most fund companies have a minimum initial deposit of $1,000 or less, and some have minimums of only $50. In addition, most fund companies lower the minimum initial deposit substantially if you agree to begin a systematic deposit program when you make your first investment.

2. Diversification If you have only a few hundred or a few thousand dollars to invest, you could barely get a single stock or bond for that dollar amount. And if the stock plummets or the bond goes into default, your money and your dreams for your child are gone.

Yet for about the same amount as the cost of a ticket at Disney World, you can get a professionally managed portfolio, consisting of partial ownership in hundreds of companies. Using a mutual fund allows even the smallest of investors to participate in the stock market, and keeps you from letting a bad choice ruin your child's future.

3. Systematic Deposit Program This mouthful of a term describes the process of saving money for your child on a regular, "autopilot" basis. The importance of starting a systematic dollar-cost averaging program is that you are avoiding one of the biggest enemies to making your kid a millionaire: *procrastination* (see "Ten Things You Need to Know," #2, page 39). By having a few dollars taken out of your checking account each month, you avoid having to remember to write the check, find a stamp and an envelope, and mail it to the fund.

This program is also helpful if you are having a hard time digging up enough money to invest for your child. Let's say you want to make your child a millionaire forty years from now, and to accomplish this you are going to invest in an account that will earn you 10% per year. You would need to deposit $22,091 today to reach $1 million in forty years.

You say you don't have that kind of money right now? No problem. Just start the account with $500, and contribute about $155 per month in a systematic deposit program, and at 10% annually you'll still reach $1 million in forty years. The mutual fund company can automatically deduct these deposits from your checking account, and you never have to lift a finger.

Even if you don't have $155 per month to save, you do have time. Lots of time. And the more time you have to establish your child's financial security, the less the systematic deposit into the mutual fund needs to be (remember the seesaw from the Introduction [see page 23]?).

4. The Power of Dollar-Cost Averaging

Making the same dollar deposit each month does not mean you are purchasing the same number of shares every time. But this can be a good thing:

Month	Deposit	Fund Price	Shares Purchased
1	$100	$5.00	20.0
2	100	5.43	18.4
3	100	5.89	16.9
4	100	4.20	23.8
5	100	4.89	20.4
6	100	4.43	22.6

What you end up doing is something that many investors know they should do but have a difficult time achieving: You are buying more shares when prices are low and less shares when prices are high. And you are doing this without having to "guess" when prices *are* high or figure out when they are low.

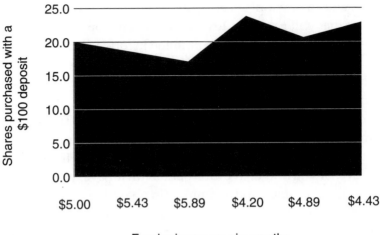

Fund prices over six months

Total: $600 purchased 122.1 shares at an average cost of $4.91 per share

5. Easy Additions and Withdrawals Most mutual funds allow direct deposits of $50 or less. This means your child can deposit proceeds from baby-sitting, an allowance, or a newspaper route. Usually there is a perforated sheet on your quarterly mutual fund statement. If you wish to add money, just tear off the bottom part of the sheet, enclose a check made payable to the fund company (with the fund account number in the "memo" line), and send it in.

This is a great time to invoke "Ten Things You Need to Know," #8 (see page 45). Sit down with your parents and in-laws, and have a conversation that goes something like this: "Mom and Dad, we want you to know how much we appreciate your being a part of our child's life. You know you don't have to buy any gifts for him. And if you do, you can buy him whatever the heck you want. But we've established this mutual fund account for his benefit.

So if you decide you would like to give him something beyond a toy or clothes, I'm sure he would appreciate it. If not now, then down the road." And don't bring up the subject again. My guess is you won't have to, and if you do need to bring it up again, they've probably already made their decision in the matter!

You can also withdraw money very quickly from these accounts. When you open the account, make sure you initial the "Telephone Redemption" part of the account application. This will give you the convenience of being able to call a toll-free number to request a redemption, and a check will be sent the next day.

Disadvantages of a Mutual Fund

1. **"I lost money *and* I owe taxes?!"** An investor who had money in any one of several technology-based funds in early 2000 ended the year in a foul mood. She checked her year-end statement and found her account value was cut in half (or worse). Then, to add insult to injury, she received a call from her tax preparer telling her that because of her fund's distribution of net realized capital gains she also owed a steep tax bill, even though the fund had, at her instruction, immediately reinvested the dividend distributions into her account.

This scenario is not common, but it does happen. If the prospect bothers you, consider a tax-advantaged fund instead. If you are investing solely for your child's retirement, you may want take a look at the variable annuities discussed in Chapter 4.

2. **What Exactly Am I Invested In?** Mutual funds are required to report their holdings once every six months. And that is just a one-time "snapshot" of what the fund held on the reporting date. During the other 363 days of the year, you will have no

way of knowing in what stocks your money is invested (although you will have a better idea if you use an index fund, because you will be able to check the current components of the index).

This ambiguity is never a problem with investors when the fund is going up in value. It's only when the fund is sinking like a stone that people start wondering exactly where their money was.

Mutual fund companies assert that if all of their buys and sells were immediately public, other investors could profit by selling or buying securities ahead of the fund. And many funds do report their holdings on a quarterly or even monthly basis. Still, if your top priority is knowing exactly where your money is at all times, you would be better off buying individual stocks and bonds.

3. Tax Accounting 101 Accumulating shares in a mutual fund through systematic dollar-cost averaging is a wonderful idea. Selling them when you or your child needs the money is also as simple as can be (see above).

The fun comes when you file a tax return after you've sold shares. You have to pay taxes on the net profits you've made. The IRS "helps" you by allowing you to figure your profit using one of the following methods:

1. FIFO (first in, first out): start with the shares you first purchased, and work your way forward. (This is the default method of the IRS)
2. Average cost: divide your total investment by the number of shares you purchased (don't forget any you bought through the reinvestment plan). You can either lump all of your shares together, or separate them according to holding periods—long- and short-term. This method is only available if you made multiple purchases at different prices, and if a custodian

(like the fund or a brokerage firm) held the shares in safekeeping.

3. Designated shares: You match certain purchases with sales, whichever generates the most advantageous gain or loss for your situation. You must specify to your broker or fund company which shares you are selling at the time of sale, and you need the confirmation of the sale in writing from the broker or fund company.

But like a lot of things in life, the flexibility of choices only complicates things further. And once you pick a particular method, you have to continue using that one until all the shares have been liquidated and the taxes have been paid.

Your situation could justify something else, but what I do is save all of my annual statements and use the FIFO method. Whenever I sell shares in the fund, I highlight the shares purchased that match the number of shares sold.

For instance, let's say you've been investing for your child for years, and you now need to pull out $1,000 for school. You call the fund, liquidate enough shares to cover the amount. On your next statement you will see a transaction that looks something like this:

125 shares sold @ $8 per share

When tax time comes, if you're using the FIFO method, you would start with your initial purchase in the fund and keep going through your subsequent purchases until you've reached 125 shares. Your cost basis of the shares you sold is the total dollar amount you paid for those 125 shares.

You can get more information from the IRS by visiting www.irs.gov and asking for Publication 564—*Mutual Fund Distributions.* Don't worry—I've never heard of anyone being imprisoned for making a mistake calculating her mutual fund cost basis. But I don't want you to be the first.

College Factor

Despite the drawbacks, mutual funds are still the primary method parents use to save for their children's college education. There are some things you should keep in mind that will help you make the most of these accounts:

1. Mutual funds held in your name or your child's name can be used for a wide variety of expenses, not just tuition costs. If you are putting money aside strictly for a college education, you should consider the Qualified State Tuition Plans profiled in Chapter 2.
2. When your child is a toddler, you can afford to be aggressive with the money, keeping it all in stock funds. As he nears high school graduation, you should reallocate the assets to a more conservative mix, using bond funds and money markets.
3. Just because your child is entering college, it doesn't mean you have to liquidate the entire account. Sell only what you need to pay tuition costs each semester. If he needs money for other expenses, you can establish an "allowance" for him via a systematic withdrawal plan at the mutual fund. Then you can have monthly checks sent to him or deposited directly in his checking account.

Getting Started

I have helped many of my clients start systematic mutual fund deposits for their children, and I began using it for Ellie as soon as we obtained a Social Security number for her. Some of my clients' reactions to the suggestion of a dollar-cost averaging program are similar. "Fifty dollars a month?" they ask. "We're stretched pretty thin right now. I don't know where we would come up with that kind of money *every month!*"

My response to them (and to you) is to do this on a trial basis. When you finish this chapter, force yourself to follow these steps:

1. Pick a Fund, Any Fund There are several funds mentioned in this chapter. If you want to delve a little deeper, the following publications and their Web sites offer more than enough coverage and search tools to find a fund that meets your criteria:

Publications	Web Site
Consumer Reports	www.consumerreports.org
Forbes	www.forbes.com
Fortune	www.fortune.com
Money	www.money.com
Morningstar	www.morningstar.com
Smart Money	www.smartmoney.com

You can also find an abundance of useful tools and information through the American Association of Individual Investors (www.aaii.com). Don't get too hung up on which fund you use. It matters less which fund you decide on; it's more important that you choose one and get started!

2. Title the Account Keep it in your name if you're not concerned about the taxes, or put it in your child's name if you're not worried about his reaching adulthood, taking control of the account, and liquidating it for purposes you don't approve of (see also Chapter 12).

3. Establish a Systematic Investment Plan Pick a dollar amount that at least meets the fund minimum, although I suggest picking a number that causes you to wince a little. Have that amount withdrawn from your checking account each month (the fund company will provide you with the forms).

Tell yourself that you will do this for three months, and then reevaluate the dollar amount and frequency of the deposits. If after three months you are sure you cannot afford to continue making the deposits, you can always decrease the dollar amount or the frequency of deposits until you have reached a schedule that is more comfortable for you (but my guess is that after three months, you won't even miss the money).

The important thing is that no matter how low you go in terms of payment and frequency, *do not stop the systematic deposit program.* It is the financial equivalent of dieting: Once you stop, it's hard to get started again.

chapter two

The Million-Dollar Education

(And the Absolute Best Way to Save for It)

*S*uppose I told you about a destination for your money that had a unique feature. Every dollar you put toward this purpose will increase the chances that your child will:

- Live longer
- Be happily married
- Be employed
- Attend religious services
- Exercise often
- Not smoke
- Maintain a healthy weight
- Get better health care
- Visit the dentist
- Contribute to a retirement plan
- Retire early
- Vote
- Perform community service
- Read more books
- Watch less television
- Participate in sports
- Wear a seat belt

Sounds like a pretty good lifelong "to do" list most of us would leave for our children. And your child will be more likely to do all of these things if she receives a college degree.

Yet it's sometimes hard to focus on your child's quality of life—or what it will be decades from now—when you're trying to find money to invest for your child's college education. Undoubtedly—and fairly enough—you'll really lose sight of these intangibles if you're trying to scare up tuition funds *while* your kid is in school!

• • •

Perhaps it will motivate you to look at saving and paying for your child's higher education with an eye toward the cold, hard, bottom-line reality: helping your child get a college degree could provide your family with the greatest return on investment you will ever experience.

According to the U.S. Census Bureau, attaining a college degree leads to hundreds of thousands of dollars more in lifetime income for women, and over a million dollars in extra earnings for men (women not only typically earn less than men but are more likely to leave the workforce for parenting responsibilities). This holds true even though college graduates start working later and retire earlier than people who don't continue their formal education past high school. Start work later, quit earlier, and still earn more money—who wouldn't want that?

In fact, the rate of return on a dollar invested toward a college education can be so high, it is only proper that it be at least partially considered as just that: an investment.

For each dollar spent on tuition, fees, and room and board over a four-year enrollment period, lifetime income is increased by $30 to $35. (Postsecondary Education OPPORTUNITIES)

At least a 30-to-1 ratio! How does that compare to other investments you might make?

Humor me for a moment.

Let's say your child is twenty-two years old today, and is graduating with a degree from a four-year public university. You spent about $40,000 on her education, which you accumulated by investing about $7,000 on the day she was born, and earning 10% annually until she enrolled in college.

And let's also assume her degree will give her about $1 million more in earnings over her working years than if she had ended her formal education after high school. If she earns that extra million dollars over a thirty-five-year career, and inflation is 3%, the boost in income is worth around $400,000 in today's dollars, earning 10% annually.

Still with me? Good. Hang in there, it's worth the effort.

You put in $7,000, and twenty-two years later your child has a degree worth $400,000. That works out to about a 20% annualized rate of return! The Dow Jones Industrial Average would have to go from 11,000 to 600,000 over twenty-two years to get the same type of gain.

Okay, there is a little bit of "voodoo economics" used in this example. There are all kinds of variables that could make the numbers in my calculations statistically meaningless. But my silly little exercise isn't too far off from what some experts have found by doing serious, bona fide research.

The Washington Research Council reported that the annual rate of return for investing a dollar toward attainment of an undergraduate degree may be as high as 13%, *adjusted for inflation.*

These experts even believe these amazing numbers are probably too low, as they worked the numbers only when paying cash for college expenses, rather than borrowing money to cover costs ("leverage," or borrowing money to buy an appreciating asset, is covered in the section on borrowing to buy a home in Chapter 10). Not included either are the other economic advantages college graduates enjoy: more comprehensive health insurance, less physical exertion at work, more free time, and more flexibility.

• • •

I'd bet that the above-mentioned statistics back up what you probably already knew: getting your child into college is a good thing. Accepting that fact, your next question probably is,

"Who is going to pay for it?" Well, unless your child grows to be seven feet tall or scores 1600 on her SATs, you need to save now, borrow later, or both.

I've helped countless parents start saving for their children's college education. Usually when I broach the subject for the first time, they tell me they are interested in investing whatever they can. But some poor souls say, "I don't want to save any money for my kid's college. Whatever we accumulate will reduce the amount of grants and scholarships she receives." One otherwise intelligent father even told me he was going to buy a fishing boat right before his kid went to college. Less cash in the father's name meant his kid would receive more "free money" to apply to tuition costs.

Or so he thought. Whether this is "whistling through the graveyard," or just plain ignorance, this attitude will not get your child closer to a college degree, nor will it garner your family any tuition assistance for which you wouldn't have already qualified.

I've talked with dozens of financial aid administrators, and they told me I could make their jobs a lot easier by drilling these two concepts into the heads of parents:

1. Most financial aid is given in the form of loans that must be repaid, not grants or scholarships.
2. Saving money for college generally will not reduce the amount of assistance your child will receive.

This might be disappointing news to you, especially if you have been eyeing the new BassMaster 5000.

• • •

Some other parents have told me they plan to borrow the money when their child needs it for college. But that's not really a "plan." Borrowing should be thought of as a last resort, only to make up the difference between what you and your child have saved, and the actual cost of her college of choice.

Besides, you don't know what types of loans will be available to you when your child goes to college, or if she will be willing to take on a mountain of debt in her own name. My guess is that about the time your child graduates from high school, you will be that much closer to retirement. Do you really want to delay your "golden years" because your money is going toward loan payments, rather than your IRA?

"No problem," you say. "It's my kid's education. She can borrow the money herself, and pay it back after she graduates."

Borrowing money to go to school is better than not going at all. But by making her get a loan, you may be jeopardizing her financial independence. The U.S. Department of Education says that about one in ten of all student-loan borrowers are currently in default, and those numbers were taken during one of the greatest economic expansions in world history!

Besides, saving money for a specific goal makes that goal more likely to be realized. My wife and I save money every month for Ellie's future college costs. With every deposit we say to ourselves, "She's going to college." By the time Ellie turns eighteen, we will have made over two hundred monthly deposits in her account and made the statement over two hundred times. In the *Wizard of Oz* Dorothy had to say "There's no place like home" only three times before she was sent back to Kansas. Not to be cocky, let's just say we like our odds.

The Absolute Best Way to Save for College

Traditionally, parents who were willing to save for college costs have been confronted with a dilemma. Put the money in the child's name (under the Uniform Transfers to Minors Act) to avoid high taxes on the earnings, and upon enrollment, the financial aid office would figure 35% of the money in the UTMA account went into the family's expected contribution each year. Plus, the money was legally the child's, and she could do whatever she wanted with it, regardless of the wishes of the parents.

If parents kept the money in their own name, however, higher taxes would eat into the annual returns, making it almost impossible to gain any ground on the inflation in college costs.

Education IRAs were the first vehicle designed for the specific goal of saving for college expenses. But these were open only to lower- and middle-income families, and annual deposits were limited to just $500 per child (since raised to $2,000). Saving that amount each year for the next eighteen years at 10% will likely get your child about one year at a private college.

A few years ago, Congress gave the individual states the right to create their own college savings accounts. The plans fell along two lines. The first were prepaid tuition plans, which allowed parents to purchase units of a college education for their children in the present day's dollars. But most of those plans were limited to in-state public schools and didn't offer a lot of flexibility.

The second kind allowed parents to invest money in mutual funds (managed by the state or a private investment firm), and use the proceeds at just about any accredited school (see below). These types of investment programs are known by two different names. Whether referred to as Section 529 plans or Qualified State Tuition Plans (QSTPs), most of the states' offerings are relatively similar. And no matter where you live, where your child lives, or where she is going to school, you can pick from just about any state's plan. You can live in Illinois, deposit money in Ohio's plan for a child who lives in New York, and eventually cash out the account to send the kid to a school in Florida.

Although many states' plans are similar, they aren't equal. There are some subtle differences in the people managing the money, the investment choices offered, and the minimum investments required. Plus, some states offer small incentives to their residents to keep the money at home, so you should check into your own state's plan before you go looking at others around the country. You can research each state's plan at www.collegesavings.org.

The common components of the plans, though, mean that with QSTPs, parents and grandparents of college-bound children now have an investment option that won't be exorbitantly taxed, or squandered by a kid who, after the torture of the SATs, has sworn off higher education.

Advantages of QSTPs

1. Tax Deferral and Tax-Free! Investments in QSTPs grow tax-deferred. Regardless of how the account performs each year, neither you nor your child will have to pay taxes. It is only when (and if) your child enters college that the money is liquidated in her name, and there is no taxation on the earnings.

2. Low Maintenance Because there is no taxation on earnings, there is no 1099 form to hunt down, no distributions of income or gain to worry about, and no tax forms to file.

3. Control The money stays in your name, with a designated child as the beneficiary. If your kid doesn't attend college, she doesn't get the money.

4. Flexibility If your child doesn't attend college or doesn't need the money you've accumulated in the QSTP, you can roll the funds into another child's account, or even that of a grandchild or cousin. You can even transfer the account into your own name, and use it to go back to school (pay attention this time!). Finally, if nobody else in your child's family is ever going to need it or you need to withdraw the funds for noneducation purposes, you pay just a 10% penalty, plus the earnings are taxed at your rate.

5. No Income Restrictions Unlike Education IRAs, deposits to QSTPs are open to parents and grandparents of all income levels, not just people whose earnings are under a specified amount.

6. Many School Options You won't be surprised to learn that the proceeds from QSTPs can be used at Harvard and Stanford. But thousands of other schools also qualify, even specialized trade and two-year programs. To get the tax benefits of a QSTP, the only school requirement is that the institution is accredited by the Department of Education. You can get a comprehensive listing of the thousands of schools that meet this qualification at www.ed.gov/offices/OSFAP/Students/apply/search.html.

7. Deposit Amounts You can make deposits up to $10,000 annually ($20,000 from a married couple) per beneficiary without incurring the gift tax. And up to $50,000 can be given ($100,000 from a married couple) if you make no more deposits during the five years after the initial deposit. The minimum deposit depends on which state plan you choose, but it's usually around $100 initially, and $25 monthly. Many plans allow you to have an amount deducted automatically from your bank account, and several fund companies let your employer set up automatic deposits to be pulled right from your paycheck!

8. Estate Planning Grandparents wishing to get money out of their estate can use the $50,000/$100,000 exemption to remove assets without incurring any gift taxes, or using their regular estate exemption. As long as the donor survives for at least five years after the gift, the money (plus the interest earned) will not be subject to estate taxes. A grandparent who has two children and four grandchildren can make QSTP deposits totaling $300,000, removing the money from a potentially taxable situation.

9. Financial Aid When your child enrolls in college and applies for financial aid, the school will calculate your Expected

Family Contribution (EFC). This is the amount of money your family will have to pony up each year before you qualify for any loans or grants from the school.

Assets in a Section 529 plan count as being owned by the parents for financial aid purposes. But as this book was going to press, the Department of Education had not clarified if the earnings *withdrawn* from a Section 529 plan would count as an asset of the parent, or as of the child, when financial aid packages were being calculated in subsequent years.

Even if the Department of Education had clarified their stance, they could change their minds again before your kid enrolls in college and you begin taking withdrawals. Suffice it to say, in the worst-case scenario, Section 529 plans will give you a tax-free way to save for your child's college education while allowing you to keep control over the money. And assets in the plan *might* not reduce your aid package (although much of the financial aid your child gets will be loans, which you or she will have to pay back anyway).

Disadvantages of QSTPs

Although for most families QSTPs are head-and-shoulders above every other college savings vehicle, that doesn't mean they're perfect. Keep the following issues in mind when using these plans:

1. Uncertainty Until 2002, withdrawals from QSTPs for qualified expenses were taxed as income at the student's rate. The tax laws were then changed so that withdrawals for college costs were free from federal and state taxes. But that could be changed *back* again, depending on the popularity of the plans and the political climate.

And it's not just the change in tax laws that you need to keep an eye on. If your child doesn't attend college and you end up not needing the money in a QSTP for your child's education expenses, you may pay some hefty taxes and penalties on the earnings in the account.

How do you decide whether to invest the money in your own name or use a QSTP? The best rule of thumb: the greater your income while you are saving and when your child attends college, the better QSTP plans will be for you and your family.

2. Locked In Although you can choose from any state's plan, you can only transfer from one plan to another once every twelve months.

It's also unlike a mutual fund or retirement account in that you usually can't transfer between investment options within the QSTP. So while you might invest aggressively for a two-year-old, you won't be able to move the money into a more conservative account when your child nears his high school graduation. This is important, as you do not want a major stock market downturn to coincide with your kid's entrance to college.

Most plans, however, do offer an "age-balancing" option, which gradually moves the whole portfolio from a majority position in equities, to a larger percentage in bonds and cash, as your child grows older. Kind of the "lazy parent's way" to effective asset allocation.

You can exercise partial control of the asset allocation by opening up one conservative account and one aggressive account for each child. At the end of each year you can direct any additional contributions to whichever account has had the biggest drop (or smallest rise). This will allow you to approach equilibrium between the values of the two accounts.

---

3. The UTMA Question When I introduce parents to QSTPs, the first thing they usually ask me is, "Can I take the money that is now in my kid's Uniform Transfers to Minors Act (UTMA) account, and put it in a QSTP?"

The answer is, "Yes, but."

Technically, money deposited into an UTMA is a completed gift to your child, and you can't take the money back out and put it under your control (see Chapter 12). As long as your chosen QSTP provider offers the option, you can open the account under the UTMA designation. But before you do, consider your options:

- **Transfer the UTMA to an UTMA-Owned QSTP** This may be a good idea if you are in a higher tax bracket, your child is very young, and you already have more than $1,500 per year in taxable earnings in the UTMA account. But upon reaching the age of majority (usually eighteen), your child can still liquidate the QSTP, pay the taxes and penalties, and spend the money printing flyers for her boyfriend's reggae band.
- **Keep the UTMA in Place and Start a New QSTP** This works best if you have a very small amount of money in the UTMA and plan on putting more in the QSTP down the road.
- **Spend the UTMA Proceeds and Start a New QSTP** You can use the UTMA as a source for some special expenditure that benefits your kid (like braces, for example) that you normally would have paid for out-of-pocket. The money you save can augment money to be deposited in the QSTP.

Getting Started

The National Association of State Treasurers organizes The College Savings Plan Network (www.collegesavings.org), which has links to the home sites of all states offering the plan. This site allows you to compare the plans from coast to coast.

For even more detailed information, visit www.savingfor college.com. This site was founded by Joseph Hurley, a CPA and an expert on QSTPs. He is also the author of the authoritative book on QSTPs called *The Best Way to Save for College*.

Finally, a company called UPromise (www.upromise.com)

credits you with dollars in a QSTP when you spend money at any of hundreds of affiliated merchants (kind of like a frequent-flier program). The service is free. And you can even enroll other friends and family members, so that their purchases will also earn money for your child's college costs. A pitch to them like this might work: "You've bought my kid's band candy and fund-raising frozen pizzas, now you can pay for her to go to Princeton!"

chapter three

When You Must Make Your Kid an Instant Millionaire

Protecting Your Child from the Financial Tragedy of Your Sudden Death

What would happen if your worst nightmare came true, and you were to die before your child reached adulthood? The chances of this occurring are small. But according to the U.S. Census Bureau, in this country there are about eight hundred thousand children under age eighteen who have a deceased parent. That's less than one in ninety, or about one kid out of three typical public school classrooms.

Some people find comfort in these types of numbers, but others mistakenly use the improbability to completely avoid addressing the issue. Although the chance of your passing away prematurely may be small, we are all aware of a situation where an untimely illness or accident has deprived a child of a parent's love, care, and financial support. Not only would your unexpected death make it much less likely that your kid would eventually become wealthy, but his very well-being might be jeopardized unless you take the proper steps to ensure he is cared for.

The mere thought of this happening to your family can paralyze you from taking action to lessen the hardship your child would face if you weren't around. But by overcoming the uneasiness brought out by the subject, you can ensure that an unforeseen tragedy that leaves your child alone will not destroy his life.

When you establish a suitable will, name a guardian, and secure adequate life insurance, you will have made great strides in protecting your child's emotional and financial future.

Your Will

I meet with dozens of families each year to discuss their financial situation. As part of my initial "fact gathering," I ask my clients if they have a will and if it has been updated recently. At first I was shocked to find out how many of these otherwise bright and informed individuals had not yet written a simple will. The majority of those who had neglected this issue were parents with small children. Ironically these parents, the people who most needed a will, were the least likely to have one. And my findings weren't unheard of—*Consumer Reports* estimates that over 70% of families do not have a proper will.

Once I became a father, I understood why some parents ignore this crucial step. Many people procrastinate when it comes to any legal or financial matter, especially one as tedious as writing a will. And the process is definitely not exciting. You'll never see a headline like, I RETIRED EARLY, LOST 30 POUNDS, AND SAVED MY MARRIAGE JUST BY WRITING A WILL.

Then there is the problem of addressing an issue that is both highly unlikely to happen, and extremely difficult to consider: your premature death. Acknowledging your own mortality is hard enough, but picturing what your young child's life would be like without you is nearly impossible. Most parents have enough short-term distractions in their lives and would rather do just about anything else instead of spending time and energy on a subject like this.

Ignoring the issue doesn't guarantee that it won't affect you and your family. Indeed, if you and your spouse die without a will, your state's probate court will begin a lengthy and expensive proceeding to decide what happens to your kid and your estate. And eventually, the actions of the state may coincide exactly with what you would have wanted for your child.

But that is unlikely.

Every family is different, and what you want to happen to your child and your assets probably varies from what your state's laws dictate. The only way you can ensure your wishes are met is by writing a will.

And it really isn't that hard, especially for the typical young family. When Ellie was born, Rachel and I decided we wouldn't go out to dinner together until we finished the process of setting up our will. And once we did finish, we "rewarded" ourselves with a nice dinner at our favorite restaurant. Needless to say, the sense of accomplishment and relief we experienced made for an enjoyable night out!

Do It Yourself

Once you have made the commitment to the task, the next step is to decide who is going to do the job. Although the obvious answer is a lawyer, you might be tempted to save a few dollars by doing it yourself. Whether you can write your own will depends on a few factors:

- Your state's laws
- The complexity of your family and financial situation
- Your ability to wade through documents filled with legal jargon

If you are in a state that allows you to do so, and are confident that your skills are strong enough to handle your simple arrangements, you can find many software programs for under a hundred dollars that allow you to take care of the matter yourself. You can learn more about the process at www.nolo.com.

But after you weigh out the costs and complexity, you might choose to hire an attorney to assist you. This is an especially good idea if you have a larger estate, because the higher your net worth, the more expensive your mistakes will be. Even a small error on your part can cost your child several thousand dollars of legal fees and hundreds of thousands of dollars in unnecessary estate taxes. You also run the risk that an omission or blunder you make will cause your nonmonetary wishes to be overruled by legal statute. The small amount of money you save by writing your own will probably will not be worth jeopardizing your plans.

Using an Attorney

As a matter of fact, if you do choose to have a lawyer help you, the most difficult step for most people is getting around to calling an attorney and setting an appointment, especially if you don't already have a relationship with a lawyer. If you are in this situation, ask your friends, family, or coworkers if they can recommend one to help you.

Having a lawyer assist you with a simple will usually costs just a few hundred dollars, and even a more complicated will and estate plan can be had for $2,000 or less. Although using an attorney doesn't guarantee your estate will pass to your heirs without a hitch, lawyers are trained to ask you the right questions and help you construct a plan that addresses your specific situation.

During your first meeting with your lawyer, you might be a little intimidated. And you may be afraid of asking the wrong questions, or being asked a question to which you don't know the answer. I have many clients who have felt this way about meeting with an adviser, and I always tell them about two irrefutable laws that apply to this situation.

First, the lawyer works for you. You are paying him for his time, and he is obligated to serve your needs in a way that makes you feel comfortable. A good attorney will not only ease your anxiety about what you are trying to do, he will also know just what questions to ask to help him do his job (which is making sure your wishes are met). He should be part therapist, part advocate, and all confidant. Like a doctor, he's seen everything, and nothing you can say will shock him. If you don't get a feeling of confidence in his abilities after the first meeting, find a new lawyer.

The second thing I tell people is that we advisers get down on our knees every night and thank heaven that you, the general public, don't know everything that we know about our respective fields of expertise. The lawyer hopes you don't know everything there is to know about writing a will; otherwise, he would be out of a job!

The basic directions you can make in your will include:

- Who gets your estate
- Who becomes the guardian of your minor child
- When your beneficiaries can gain access to their share of your estate
- Who becomes the personal representative for your estate

You can also use this opportunity to make more detailed directions, such as designating that a certain piece of your property go to a specific relative. And most attorneys will explain and help you establish a Living Will, Durable Power of Attorney, and a Health Care Power of Attorney.

Naming an Executor

You should use this opportunity to name a personal representative of your estate, also known as an executor. The executor is required to administer your estate through probate (the legal process in which all your bills are paid, taxes are addressed, and property is passed to your intended beneficiaries). When all of this is accomplished, the executor's obligation is through.

Because this can be a difficult and time-consuming job, you should choose your executor carefully. First, she should be a person who not only knows you well but also has a decent background in financial and legal matters. Ask if she is willing to serve in this capacity, and don't be disappointed if she turns you down. Even if she agrees to your request, you should also name an alternate executor in case your first pick changes her mind or is otherwise prevented from doing the job. Once you complete your will, make sure you tell the executor where the will is stored—a safe or safety deposit box is your best choice. Your lawyer will also maintain a copy at his office.

Your Child's Guardians

This is often the most sensitive part of the process for parents. You are going to ask someone to serve in your capacity as parents until your child reaches adulthood—a tremendous honor, and an enormous obligation. You may already have people in mind who are willing to serve. If not, consider the following issues:

- Do the people share your beliefs and values?
- How old (and energetic) will they be when your kid is a teenager?
- If you are asking a husband and wife, do they have a relatively stable relationship?
- Do they have children similar in ages to yours?
- If so, does your kid get along with theirs?

Don't overlook the issue of location, either. The grief your child will experience may be softened if he can remain in his community, with the same school, friends, and social circle.

Another concern for you should be the economic situation of the potential guardians. Are they relatively well off, or will taking care of your child create a financial burden for them? You should definitely consider this issue when you are deciding how much money your child would need if you weren't around. Having sufficient assets to use for your kid may increase the likelihood that your ideal candidates will agree to serve as guardians for your child. You should make them aware that you have taken steps to ensure that caring for your child will not create a financial hardship for their family.

Understand that this is a delicate matter, and one that you don't want to damage a close relationship. Once you are ready to approach suitable friends or family members, make it clear when you ask them that they have the right to decline, and if they do there will be no hard feelings. Even if they do accept, you should tell them that they can change their minds at any time, and you will respect their wishes.

If you are having a difficult time finding a willing and appropriate guardian, you may want to follow in the steps of a couple I worked with. They didn't live near any family members, and in the interest of continuity, they wanted to be sure their children would remain in the same geographic area. The parents and kids were close to another family in their neighborhood who had children of similar ages. During a ski trip with this family, my clients related their struggles to find the right guardian. It turned out the other family was in the same situation, and within a few days the couples had agreed to serve as guardians for each other's kids.

If you meet your untimely demise, your choice of guardian is not final. As one more "safety net" designed to protect your child, in the event of your death the guardian must be approved by the court. This process is usually easily achieved, but the court can reject the guardian if it finds strong evidence that your original selection wouldn't be in the child's best interests.

Determining the Financial Needs of Your Child

After you have prepared your will and found appropriate guardians, your next step is to make sure that all the financial needs of your child and their guardians will be met.

How much money should you leave to your child? The insurance industry rule of thumb is anywhere from five to seven times the parents' annual pretax income. But from a purely financial standpoint, I happen to think you are worth a lot more than that.

Why? Because of the paychecks you and your spouse are going to receive over the life of your child. That income stream has a value today that is much higher than you might imagine.

(This paragraph is going to make your heart race and your breathing difficult, so brace yourself.) My personal rule of thumb for providing for an orphaned child is you should have $40,000 in assets left to your child for each year he is under the age of twenty-five. That means I believe parents of a newborn baby should have at least $1 million of net estate value left to their child.

Are you okay? This sounds like an incredibly high number. But don't worry, later in this chapter I'll show how you can reach it with surprisingly affordable term life insurance.

Replacing even a moderate income over the lifetime of a child costs more than you probably realize. Let's say your gross annual household income is $75,000, and that number is going to go up each year at the level of inflation. Assuming you're going to work for another twenty-five years and annual inflation is 3%, you would need to leave your child *$1,072,000* earning 8% per year to replace that income and maintain his quality of life. Maybe this astounding revelation of the current economic value of your job will help you drag yourself out of bed on Monday mornings.

And when you look at the total costs associated with raising a typical child, include the expense of making sure that your child's guardians can afford to give him all the attention and support he needs; and finally, after you add in a generous allowance for college and other expenses, a million dollars for a newborn baby starts to make more sense:

1. General Expenses According to the U.S. Department of Agriculture, a child born in 2000 will cost a middle-income family $233,000 in inflation-adjusted dollars, just from the child's birth until he reaches the age of eighteen. An "upper-income" family (defined in the report as a family making more than $64,000 pretax annual income in 2000—I wonder how many families at this level feel that they are "upper-income"?) will spend about $340,000 in inflation-adjusted dollars to raise a child over the same time period.

2. Subsidizing Your Guardians' Expenses Recently Rachel and I were asked to serve as potential guardians for two children of a family we know. We thought about it and agreed. Afterward, the parents told us only half-jokingly, "Don't worry about money. If we die, these kids are going to be filthy rich." Not the determining factor in our decision, but it was nice to know the parents had realized the financial implications of caring for their children.

You want to make the guardians' job as easy as possible. Do you want your child's guardians to be forced to put your kid in day care, or would you like one of the guardians to be able to stay home to care for your (and their) child? Perhaps a nanny would be more appropriate. How about the guardians' home? They might need to buy a new house so your kid can have his own bedroom. If your child wants to go to camp, for example, can the guardians afford to send their kids, too? And don't forget that your child may eventually have some unusual medical expenses.

Depending on your priorities and situation, the total of these extra expenses could run close to $3,000 per month for eighteen years. At 3% inflation, that might require about *$450,000* at the birth of the child.

3. College Expenses In 2001 the College Board estimated that four years of tuition, room, and board at a four-year private college costs about $90,000. If these costs escalate at an annual rate of 5%, a four-year private education might cost over $215,000 eighteen years from now. You should have a minimum of

$100,000 of estate value for an undergraduate education, and more if you would like to make sure he can attend a postgraduate program.

4. Life After College The first three expense categories should take your child into adulthood, which may be sufficient for you. But if you want to give your child a nest egg he can use to buy a house or start a business, you will probably need an extra $100,000 in your estate for these extra goals.

Together, these numbers would add up to the following required estate net worth for a newborn baby:

General expenses	**$ 350,000**
Guardians' expenses	**450,000**
College expenses	**100,000**
Life after college	**100,000**
Total	**$1,000,000**

You might think the interest from this money would more than pay for all of these expenses. But inflation, market volatility, and taxes will eat away at the principal quickly. If you leave a newborn baby with $1 million, earning 8% before taxes, and inflation is 3% annually, spending $50,000 after taxes (adjusted for inflation) each year will wipe out the entire amount by the time the child turns twenty-five.

Your actual numbers may be more or less than this, depending on a few factors:

- *The age of your child*   The older he is, the less money you need
- *Other sources of financial support*   Like grandparents or the guardians
- *The cost of where your child will live*   South Dakota or Silicon Valley?

Once you have decided how much money your child will need, you should compute what your monetary worth would be if you and your spouse died today. You can calculate your current estate's net worth through the following basic formula:

Assets	(House, IRA, life insurance, investments)
−Liabilities	(Mortgage, other debts, estate taxes)
Net estate	

When you have attained this number, you can figure what the gap is between how much you have and how much your kids would need if you were to die today. To be safe, I use the age of twenty-five as an age that your child will no longer need any support from you. Again, I believe a conservative amount for each child's share of your estate should be $40,000 for every year he is under the age of twenty-five (25 × $40,000 = $1,000,000).

For example, let's say you have a six-year-old son and a ten-year-old daughter, and a current net estate of $300,000. Your gap in coverage would look like this:

Daughter:	(25−10) × $40,000 = $ 600,000
Son:	(25−6) × $40,000 = $ 760,000
Initial total	$1,360,000
Minus current estate	− 300,000
Potential shortfall	$1,060,000

The best way to bridge this shortfall is by purchasing life insurance on the lives of you and your spouse.

Filling the Gap with Life Insurance

Life insurance is a very necessary tool to protect your family's future. But mention the topic to many people, and their first reaction is eye-rolling skepticism. And to some extent, this response is justified. Some insurance companies and agents have exaggerated the positive aspects of policies, and the aggressive tactics of a few insurance agents have caused a backlash from both the general public and the financial media. Although I have held an insurance license for many years, I never sold a policy, and had a strong degree of cynicism toward many people who did sell insurance.

But a few years ago my eyes were opened as to just how important an adequate amount of life insurance can be. A man whom I had known for a few years was stricken with cancer. He was in his early thirties, married, and had two children. A loving and caring husband and father, and a hardworking professional, he never expected anything like this disease to enter into his life. The initial outlook was not good, but there was reason for hope.

Shortly after his diagnosis, he and I had a conversation about his situation. We discussed his treatment schedule, how his wife was coping, and how the disease was affecting his ability to perform his job. Although his life had been knocked into complete disarray, he was strong enough to discuss these issues in an even tone of voice. But when he began talking about his kids, his voice became choked with emotion and fear. Tears streamed down both our faces as he discussed the possibility of not being able to watch them grow up. I was single at the time with no kids of my own, but his sadness over the loss his family might experience was the most powerful example I had ever witnessed of the love a father can feel for his children.

Before we parted, he told me something I never forgot. He said, "Remember this when you have kids of your own. My brother used to work for an insurance company, and he always encouraged us to buy as much life insurance as we could afford. I was skeptical about how good an idea this was, but I went along with his suggestions. After he stopped working there, I planned to cancel most of the insurance, but I never got around to it. The only good thing about this illness is because of that insurance, my wife and kids will miss me, but not my paycheck."

He put up a valiant fight, but eventually the cancer overtook him and he died. At his funeral, I watched the pallbearers wheel the casket down the aisle of the church. The man's young children slowly walked behind, sobbing quietly. It was the most heartbreaking thing I had ever seen.

Yet as I watched his children, I couldn't help but think that although their father was gone, he wasn't going to stop providing for them. I realized then that we can't control how long we will be around for our children, but through the appropriate use of life insurance, we can make sure our kids don't suffer if we can't give them our financial support.

Types of Life Insurance

Life insurance policies fall into two broad categories: term and cash value. Cash-value policies (like whole, universal, or variable life insurance) are part investment account, part death protection. Term life insurance, on the other hand, provides only the death benefit.

There has been a fierce debate among advocates of each of these types of coverage. Proponents of term insurance point to much lower premiums, the greater ability to pinpoint specific needs with term insurance, the high commissions cash-value polices generate for life insurance agents, and the sometimes-misleading numbers quoted by these salespeople.

But cash-value boosters also have a case. Cash-value life insurance might be for you if:

- You don't mind paying higher commissions for the help of an agent
- You don't trust yourself to save money through more economical investment methods, like mutual funds
- You need more flexibility than a term policy can offer

There is a certain amount of truth to both sides. But deciding what type of insurance is best for you is no different from weighing any other financial issue. You need to first identify your goals, and then decide which course of action best addresses those goals. In this case we are talking solely about pro-viding your child with a replacement for a premature loss of his parents' income. And term life insurance provides the most cost-efficient method to obtain the adequate amount of cover-age needed to meet this goal.

Unlike cash-value life insurance, which remains in force until the policy is liquidated or you die, term insurance gets its name because it offers coverage only for a specified term of your choosing, usually from one to twenty years. Once the time period is up, the relationship between you and the insurance company is over. You don't need to pay any more premiums, but you also won't have any insurance.

But that's fine, and it shows why term is perfect for provid-ing for your kid. You won't need insurance any longer than this, because you hopefully have chosen a period of coverage that will expire exactly when your child has stopped relying on your income. For example, say you have a ten-year-old, and you want to protect him from the loss of your support until he turns twenty-five. You and your spouse can buy a fifteen-year term policy on your lives, with a death benefit equal to what he would need to survive and thrive.

The sense of using term versus cash value for this purpose is readily apparent when you weigh the cost of each option. Let's say you have two children, ages five and ten. You and your spouse agree you need to purchase $1 million of life insurance on yourselves for each child, to bridge the gap between what you're currently worth and what your child would need. Based on your assets, you decide you need insurance until the kids turn twenty (after that, you've calculated that your estate should be large enough to take care of their needs). For your ten-year-old, you will purchase $500,000 of ten-year term in-surance on the lives of both you and your spouse. Your five-year-old will need the same amount for a fifteen-year term.

According to the insurance Web site Quotesmith (www.quotesmith.com), a healthy thirty-five-year-old man and woman, of normal height and weight, can purchase four term policies for the following amounts:

Child	Insurance	Monthly Premium
Ten-year-old	$ 500,000 (mother)	$15
	500,000 (father)	20
Five-year-old	500,000 (mother)	20
	500,000 (father)	30
Total	$2,000,000	$85

The numbers in this example are staggering. The insurance proceeds would completely protect these children from elementary school into adulthood, all for less than the cost of taking a family of four to a ballgame!

• • •

Finding out what a similar amount of cash-value insurance will actually cost isn't quite as simple. First of all, the cold truth about life insurance is that it is a bet. You are gambling with the insurance company. If you purchase term insurance, the insurance company easily calculates how likely it is that someone of your height, weight, and health condition will die during the coverage period, adds on enough to make a profit, and sets the premium accordingly. If it's any consolation to you, the insurance company would like nothing more than for you to live forever, or at least a day past the expiration of your term insurance.

But when you purchase cash-value life insurance, you get to keep the coverage in force for as long as you pay the premiums. And the premiums can either be fixed or variable (and tied to the investment performance of the account).

The variance between when you might die and how much you will have paid in premiums by the *time* you die makes the insurance company's calculations a little trickier. It is more difficult for them to predict the timing of your death over many decades than it is to guess if you'll survive for ten or fifteen years. And the older you get, the better the chance that you will die, obligating the insurance company to pay the death benefit. So they charge higher premiums than term initially to make up for the uncertainty, and hope that you live a long and happy life.

The comparison between the costs of fixed cash-value premiums and term costs usually looks something like this:

The first step to finding out the cost of cash-value life insurance is to contact a reputable agent. A good way to make even the most decent insurance salesperson salivate is to call him up and tell him you are interested in purchasing a million dollars of cash-value life insurance. My guess is that by time you hang up the phone, he will be knocking at your door with a computer illustration in his hand.

The problem with this illustration is that it is hypothetical. The insurance company has used their best guess to factor in what interest and earnings they will earn on your premiums over the life of the policy. But if you've ever taken out a mortgage, you know interest rates can fluctuate wildly and are difficult to predict (this goes double for the stock market). If the insurance company uses an excessive rate of return in their policy illustration, and the actual rate of return is lower than projected, you will end up paying even more than the premium amount in the illustration.

Even if the interest rate projection is accurate, the quoted premium for a cash-value policy will be much higher than a term policy of equal face value because of the commissions paid to insurance salespeople. Most good insurance agents will admit they make much more from selling cash-value life insurance than they do from term policies. Some insurance companies pay up to 70% of your first year of cash-value life premiums to the agent, and then the agent gets a smaller percentage of the premiums as long as you keep paying them.

There is nothing wrong with this, as good insurance agents need to make a living just like everybody else. But if the couple in the previous example were to try to arrive at their $2 million target with whole life instead of term, their premium could be well over $400 per month, compared to $85 for the same type of term coverage. And that $400 would only get them "second-to-die" insurance—there would be a payoff only when both parents passed away. With the term insurance, either parent's dying would generate $1 million for the remaining spouse and children.

Some agents point out that a downside of term insurance is the issue of "renewal." This means that when term insurance expires, you have to prove your insurability all over again to be able purchase more insurance. But there are two reasons this shouldn't deter you from using term insurance to protect your child:

1. If you timed your term correctly, your child won't need your support anymore and it won't matter if you are uninsurable.

2. You can purchase a "guaranteed renewability" rider on your term policy that will permit you to renew your policy at the end of the term, with no health examination required.

The best way around the issue of renewability, though, is to pick a term that covers your child well into early adulthood. If your need for the insurance diminishes or runs out before the term is up, you can either stop paying the premiums, or lower the death benefit (and premium) to an amount that fits your situation.

A great and blessed event for you and your family would be that the term insurance will expire unused, and your premium payments will be completely wasted (although the insurance company will tell you that you purchased "peace of mind," and they have a good point).

But if the worst thing happens and your minor children become premature beneficiaries of your estate and life insurance proceeds, you probably wonder how you can prevent them from squandering the money after you're gone.

Protecting Your Child from Himself

The last steps in preparing for the premature death of you and your spouse are to make sure your child doesn't take control of your estate before he is capable of responsibly managing all that money. By creating a trust as part of your will, you can avoid letting your teenage child become an unsupervised millionaire.

Which is exactly what he will become if you choose not to create a trust. If you and your spouse die, your minor child will inherit your estate. The good news is that if he is a minor, the law will not allow him to actually receive the money. The funds will go into a guardianship or UTMA/UGMA (minor's) account, to be looked after by an adult chosen by you in your will or appointed by the court after your death. The bad news is that when your child reaches the age of eighteen (or twenty-one, depending on your state) the guardianship or UTMA/UGMA accounts are taken over by your kid. Immediately. And there is nothing you, the guardians, or the court can do to stop him from throwing the graduation party to end all graduation parties.

Establishing a Trust

That is why most parents use a trust when leaving larger sums of money to their children. Unlike an UTMA/UGMA or guardianship account, a trust can allow for a gradual release of the assets, giving your child more discretion over the money as he (hopefully) becomes more mature. You can even prevent him from getting complete authority over the assets until he reaches his thirties. The issue of control over the money is covered more thoroughly in Chapter 12, but the basic principles will demonstrate what a prudent idea a trust can be.

Your attorney can help you create the trust when you write your will. Depending on the complexity of your will and trust, this will add another few hundred or few thousand dollars to your legal costs, but it is money well spent. The trust can remain unfunded until you and your spouse have both passed away, and then the trust becomes the owner of your assets and life insurance with your child as the beneficiary.

The trust becomes your tool to manage how your child and his guardians spend the money you have left behind, with the trustee acting as a "gatekeeper." The issues you may want to address in the trust document are wide-ranging, but some common ones include:

1. Maintenance This is a monthly payment to your child's guardians to offset expenses like food and clothing.

2. Health Care You should authorize the guardians to spend whatever amount necessary to meet your child's medical needs.

3. Education College and graduate studies are an obvious goal, but don't forget about tuition for a private elementary and secondary school.

4. Guardians You may want to help the guardians buy a larger house, work less, or pay for some benefits for their biological children.

In addition to addressing specific needs, you may also want to "reward" milestones in your child's life, such as giving him a larger amount when he graduates from college, gets married, buys a home, or has a child.

Be very specific about the exact conditions in which your child should get the money. I knew a man who, as a teenager, lost his father. The father's lawyer made it very clear that the father had left the young man some money, but the only way the teenager could get the money was to go to college right after high school. The young man looked over the will carefully and determined he merely had to *enroll* in college to get the entire sum. Upon graduating from high school, he signed up at the local university, took his admissions slip down to the lawyer's office, and picked up the check. He then immediately dropped out of college and bought a Corvette with the father's money.

This type of audacity later served the man well, as he went on to have a very successful business career. But I don't think one day of college was what his father had in mind when he wrote the will.

You don't have to limit the release of assets to your child's achievements. Most trusts have a minimum age at which the child takes the reins. But rather than giving your child an "all-or-nothing" date to get the money, I like the idea of splitting the money into portions and releasing it over time (see Chapter 12). This way he will hopefully learn how to handle the assets by the time he gets the last and largest sum.

Choosing a Trustee

Whether you choose to use an UTMA/UGMA account or a trust to hold the assets, you should use your will to name someone to act as a custodian or trustee for these accounts until your child takes control. If you choose a trust, you then need to designate a trustee to manage the assets until the child takes over. You can name an individual, an institution, or a combination of the two as cotrustees.

Your first inclination may be to name the guardians of your child as the trustee. After all, if you have confidence in the guardians' ability to look after your kid, why can't these people also handle your child's money? For simplicity's sake you may choose this route, but there are two important reasons you should consider having someone other than the guardians serve as trustee.

The first issue is the skills required of a trustee. A person acting in this capacity should have a good head for business and money, a long-term perspective, and the wisdom to recognize when to get involved and when to step back. You should consider your child fortunate if you can find loving people willing to serve as guardians. But it may be nearly impossible to find someone who not only meets your criteria for taking care of your child but also has the knowledge, time, and interest required to serve as trustee.

The second issue involved is the "fox and the henhouse" problem. You hope the guardians will always act in your child's best interests. But sometimes people change, and your guardians may be tempted to take advantage of the tremendous level of trust you have given them. A separate, unbiased trustee can prevent the guardians from depleting your child's assets for things that don't fit with the goals you had in mind. And even if the guardians are only spending the money in a way they think is best for your child, a third party monitoring the process can prevent even the appearance of any conflict of interest.

Choosing an individual to serve as a third-party trustee is almost as difficult (and important) as choosing guardians for your kid. You may have the luxury of a close friend or relative who has the necessary skills to handle the tax, legal, and investment aspects of overseeing a trust. This person may be a good choice if you would like the trustee to know you and your child well, as an intimate knowledge of your family can help this person make the choices you would have made.

But there are drawbacks to choosing the friend or relative. The trustee may have to make some tough choices, and will sometimes need to tell your child "No." This may alienate your kid from the trustee, and make the trustee wish he never had agreed to accept the job. And if this individual is unable or unwilling to serve as trustee, an appropriate successor trustee may have to be appointed by the courts, and you won't be around to give your input to the decision.

A more common choice as trustee is an institution, such as a bank. A bank's trust department has many "checks and balances" in place to make sure the money is managed appropriately and that your wishes are met. Continuity is not an issue, because regardless of turnover or personnel changes, the bank will always have an interest in serving as trustee. Why? Because they will charge the trust a fee of around 1% of assets each year. This is a strong incentive to keep the assets under their management!

The best choice may be to have a trusted friend or relative serve as cotrustee with a bank, and plan on paying that person for their services. This way your child will have the benefit of a familiar person watching the assets combined with the continuity and skills offered by an institution. And you can give your child and your individual cotrustee the right to fire the bank as cotrustee, as long as they replace it with a similar type of institution.

College Factor

It will be difficult enough to get your child a college education if you *are* around to pay for it. If you and your spouse die prematurely, the amount of debt and work your child will have to endure may make it virtually impossible for your kid to go to college if you haven't planned in advance. Your deaths would bring a severe amount of emotional pain to your child, but by planning effectively you can foster your child's intellectual development even after you're gone.

Getting Started

1. If you have a minor child and you don't yet have a will, call an attorney today and make an appointment. He will be able to get you on the road to protecting your child.

2. Be thinking about potential guardians before the meeting with the lawyer, and he may be able to help you make the decision.

3. He should mention the idea of creating a trust to hold your assets, but if he doesn't, it is okay to ask his opinion.

4. While you are in his office, ask him if he will help you calculate your present estate's net worth.

5. Once you have determined your needs, call your insurance agent to ask about purchasing additional term insurance on the lives of you and your spouse, matching the coverage length with the time until your child will be in his early twenties. Compare the quotes the agent gives you with those found at these sites:

www.quotesmith.com
www.insweb.com
www.quickeninsurance.com

Finally, you should review your wills, trusts, and insurance every three to five years. Your family, finances, and guardian choices can change, and an update may prevent additional suffering by your child if you die while he is a minor.

PART TWO
Ages Seven Through Twelve

Now you're into the "rapid growth" years. Not only is your child developing quicker than you ever could have imagined, but the cost of raising a kid is really starting to kick in, especially if you have more than one. Hopefully, you've already written a will (if it's more than five years old, have you reviewed it lately?) and made sure you have enough life insurance to support your child, no matter what happens.

And you should definitely have a QSTP account going, for your oldest child at least (you can always roll part of the proceeds into the names of your younger children if your oldest doesn't need it). As a matter of fact, at the end of this period your main goal should be making sure there is enough money for your first child to go to college.

If you have a little left over and still qualify, a Roth IRA for yourself is one of the best things you can do for your family's financial flexibility. And with the many decades you have until your child's retirement, a few thousand dollars in a variable annuity can still go a long way toward securing your kid's golden years.

Finally, your child is probably starting to make purchases on his own. Not only is this a prime opportunity to begin teaching him to save his allowance and form a budget, but you can also explore the possibility of buying stock in some of the companies that are on the *receiving* end of his dollars.

chapter four

The Instant Retirement Account

Low-Hassle, Tax-Deferred Growth for Your Child

Figure out how old your child is going to be in the year 2036. That is when some experts predict Social Security will officially be wiped out. The enormous baby-boom generation will have retired to Florida by then, their collective weight creating a danger that the state will break off at Georgia and start floating toward Cuba.

According to some calculations, by then retired Americans will have withdrawn the money from the Social Security program faster than the younger workers can replenish it. And if you think any politician is going to reduce payments to baby boomers just to keep the system afloat, then I find your innocence and purity refreshing. But you are probably wrong.

Even if you are right, the chances that your child will be able to count on government payments to retire comfortably are almost nonexistent. Portions of this book are devoted specifically to ensuring that your kid's "golden years" will be a time of ease and contentment for her. Chapter 5 (your Roth IRA), Chapter 8 (your child's Roth IRA), and Chapter 9 (your child's 401[k]) give you three powerful options to provide your child with sufficient income during the postemployment period of her life.

But each of these choices has at least one drawback. Contributions to a Roth IRA are limited to a few thousand dollars per year, and converting your regular IRA to a Roth IRA can mean a big tax bill. And your child must have earned income to make IRA or Roth IRA contributions in the first place.

Finally, even if your child is working, you can't force her to contribute to her 401(k) plan. Even if you could, to reach $1 million in her retirement plan at age 65, your child would have to contribute about $160 per month over a forty-year career, and earn 10% annually on the money. That $160 might be a drop in the bucket if she gets a high-income job, but it could also be an impossible number to set aside if she is in the ranks of the overworked and underpaid.

No matter how young your child is, or whether or not she is earning income, you still have an easy way to give her a head start on a comfortable retirement, without the use of an IRA or 401(k). The investment vehicle is called an "annuity," and you will be especially interested in a type known as a "variable annuity."

First, let's describe what an annuity is. Annuities are offered by insurance companies, and the accounts are basically "jars" that contain investments (like mutual funds) similar to IRAs and 401(k)s. Annuities are also similar to retirement plans in that the earnings accumulate without being taxed. Then, upon withdrawal, any appreciation is taxed as ordinary income to the annuitant (your child). In other words, only when you take the money out of the jar will Uncle Sam be standing by with his hand out.

And another resemblance to retirement plans is that any withdrawals of earnings from an annuity before your child turns 59½ can be subject to an IRS penalty of 10%, along with the applicable state and federal taxes on the earnings.

When you deposit money into an annuity, you are entering into an agreement with the insurance company. You are giving them your money to invest on your behalf, and the rate of return the insurance company will pay you depends at least partially on what kind of annuity you choose: fixed or variable.

Fixed Annuity

A fixed-rate annuity pays you a rate of return that you agree upon before you invest, similar to a certificate of deposit (6% annually, for example). And like CDs, that rate is usually guaranteed for a certain period of time—say, five years. But unlike CDs, you don't pay taxes on the interest that stays in the fixed annuity—only when you take the interest out.

Another difference between CDs and fixed-rate annuities is that the latter are not FDIC insured. Instead, fixed-rate annuities are guaranteed by the claims-paying ability of the insurance company. Although the financial strength of insurance companies has usually been very strong, you should check the safety rating of any insurer before you fork over your money. A. M. Best (www.ambest.com) is a private company that issues ratings on most larger insurance companies. Their scale is as follows:

Rating	Definition
A++ and A+	Superior
A and A−	Excellent
B++ and B+	Very good
B and B−	Fair
C++ and C+	Marginal
C and C−	Weak
D	Poor
E	Under regulatory supervision
F	In liquidation
S	Suspended

Most companies are rated in the top one or two categories. If you are thinking of buying a fixed-rate annuity from an insurance company rated lower than "B+," you will be better off assembling your family in the backyard on a beautiful summer day and directing them to help you tear your money into little pieces. Not the classic example of "quality time," but the end result will be the same, and at least your kids will have a good story to tell for years to come.

A fixed annuity from a strong insurance company will protect your child from a loss of principal. And if the idea of the value of the account occasionally dropping below your initial deposit amount makes you nauseous, a fixed annuity might be the best option for you.

Variable Annuity

But with the long time frame you have until your child's retirement, you may be more interested in a variable annuity. Variable annuities are basically mutual funds (see Chapter 1) in an insurance wrapper. The insurance company offers several types of investment accounts within an annuity, ranging from conservative bond and money market funds to aggressive technology and emerging markets stock funds. The insurance company may manage the money themselves, but most choose to outsource the investment management to some of the widely recognized fund management companies, such as Fidelity, American Funds, or Vanguard.

Variable annuities offer a rate of return that fluctuates, depending on the type of investment option you choose. Like stocks and stock mutual funds, the values of most accounts within the variable annuity go up, and they also go down. For accepting this uncertainty about short-term performance, your child will be rewarded with a long-term rate of return that will likely be greater than what a fixed annuity would pay.

Traditionally, variable annuities have been most popular with people who are nearing retirement age, and are looking to augment their IRAs and work-sponsored plans with more flexible tax-deferred savings vehicles. But there are inherent factors in variable annuities that can make them ideal for parents who want a simple way to ensure a comfortable future for their children.

As a matter of fact, if you deposit as little as $5,000 in a variable annuity for a newborn baby, and that account achieves a net annual growth rate of 10%, by the time your baby is 65 she will have an account worth over $2.4 million! And best of all, neither you nor she will owe any taxes on the amount until the money is withdrawn.

Advantages of a Variable Annuity

1. Delaying and Deferring Taxes The real power behind using a variable annuity to make your kid a millionaire in retirement is twofold. Most important, of course, is time. But also of use to your child is another tool—tax deferral. Because annuities are classified as insurance products meant for retirement funding, the IRS treats all earnings and dividends as they do those of an IRA or a 401(k). Unlike mutual fund owners, holders of annuities pay no taxes on interest and capital gains until the money is withdrawn.

Delaying the taxes on earnings will provide little benefit when your child is young. If money were to be invested in your child's name but outside of an annuity, in 2002 the first $750 of annual earnings would be tax-free, and the next $750 would be taxed at the child's low rate, until she reaches age 14. After that age, all the earnings would be taxed at her rate.

However, the benefits of tax deferral really kick in once your child reaches adulthood and begins earning enough income to push her up into the higher tax brackets. Ideally, an annuity will help her avoid high taxation of investment earnings during this accumulation period. Then, when she reaches retirement age, she can withdraw the proceeds from the annuity at her presumably lower tax bracket.

And even if your child's tax bracket isn't a whole lot lower during her retirement, the ability to keep all earnings reinvested in the account during her accumulation period, rather than withdrawing a portion of them annually to pay the tax bill, can have a dramatic effect on your child's wealth, especially over decades of ownership.

For a purely hypothetical example of this effect, say you put $5,000 into a mutual fund for a newborn baby. Assume the account distributes 10% per year. In the interest of simplicity, figure that because of the child's low tax rate, she will pay no taxes on the distributions during her first twenty-one years, and 25% tax on the distributions each year from the ages of 21 to 65.

Then compare the first account to instead investing the money in a tax-deferred account (like an annuity) that offers the same 10% annual distributions. Figure the account is liquidated when the child turns 65, and all earnings are taxed at 35%. The approximate end result of the two accounts would look like this:

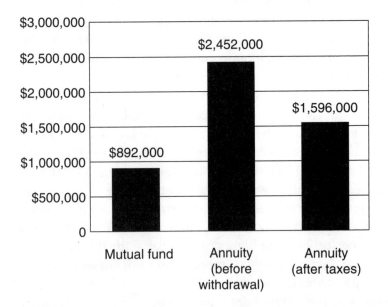

This example is not perfect. It ignores the fact that an account outside of an annuity (like a mutual fund) will rarely pay out all of its annual earnings, as some of the earnings will be applied against realized losses, reducing the amount distributed to shareholders. And a portion of the distributions will come in the form of long-term gains that are currently taxed at a lower rate than income and short-term gains. Suffice it to say that under today's tax laws, a mutual fund that distributes little or no income or short-term gains and also hangs on to most of its long-term gains will provide a better after-tax return than an equal account within a variable annuity.

But as was discussed in Chapter 1, each year a mutual fund is required to distribute all of its net gains and income. These distributions are taxable to your child even if the money is immediately reinvested into the mutual fund. This law creates a double whammy when a fund has a down year, yet must distribute net gains and income. Your child will have lost money in the year, yet still owe taxes! This "insult added to injury" can be avoided by using a variable annuity.

2. No Income Needed Despite all the similarities between annuities and IRAs or 401(k)s, there is one important difference: your child doesn't need any earned income to qualify for a deposit into an annuity. You can open an account on behalf of an infant, as long as she has a Social Security number. The minimum investment is usually no more than a few thousand dollars, and you can set up systematic deposits from a checking account for as little as $50 per month, depending on the annuity contract. You can also contribute to the annuity whenever you wish by simply sending a deposit directly to the insurance company, again usually for a minimum of $50 or so.

This ability to easily begin your child's retirement plan well before she has any earned income is a powerful jump start. Putting $5,000 at birth into a variable annuity will give your child the same amount as if she made $5,000 deposits *each year* into her 401(k) from the ages of 24 until 65 (over $200,000 of contributions!), assuming a 10% annual return.

3. Simplicity Because there is no taxation of gains and interest until the money is withdrawn, you and your child will never go through the headache of calculating the taxes due on what will initially be only small amounts of realized appreciation and income. Most other investments will incur some form of declarable interest or distribution every year, requiring you to account for the money on the child's annual tax return.

Critics of annuities marvel at how many investors choose to put money into the vehicles, despite overall expenses that are usually higher than a similar mutual fund. And the detractors have a good point. But one thing the cynics forget is that investors are human. As such, they like things to be as uncomplicated and hassle-free as possible. Combine those features with the opportunity to delay the pain of taxation into the future, and it is easier to understand why people put hundreds of millions of dollars into annuities each year.

4. Advantages over a 401(k) or IRA Once your child begins working she should not make any additional deposits to the variable annuity until all her 401(k), IRA, and Roth IRA options have been fully utilized. But if she is fortunate enough to have additional money to invest after she has maxed out her traditional retirement plans, certain features can make a variable annuity even more attractive than a 401(k) or IRA, including:

- There is no limit to additional deposits to a variable annuity
- IRS regulations require mandatory distributions to begin by the time the IRA or 401(k) owner reaches the age of 70½. But there are no government requirements to begin withdrawals from an annuity, only those from the insurance company (which usually start by age 85 or 90).

5. Multiple Investment Options Most variable annuities today offer dozens of investment options within a particular account. This means an investor can stay under the umbrella of the original annuity contract, yet still move from aggressive to conservative, from bonds to stocks and from domestic to international investments at any time, with no cost and no taxes (again, until the money is finally taken out of the annuity). This feature helps alleviate the need to move from one annuity to another (and possibly generating a "redemption fee"—the charge some companies hit you with if you take money out of an annuity during the initial years of ownership, as described in the prospectus), if the child's investment objectives change.

The opportunity to move money from one account with no cost and no taxation means that you and your child have no obstacle to rebalancing the portfolio, discussed in Chapter 9.

Sometimes the features and benefits offered by your child's annuity may not be competitive with other, newer offerings from insurance companies (for instance, there aren't enough good funds offered by the annuity, or the annual expenses are too high).

If you wish to transfer the annuity to a new provider, you can do so via a "Section 1035" exchange allowed by the IRS. This allows the assets to be moved; yet because it doesn't count as a withdrawal, there will still be no tax on the gains or income until your child eventually takes possession of the funds.

But because the new contract may bring a new schedule of redemption fees, and perhaps higher annual expenses, a Section 1035 exchange should only be made when there is a dramatic difference between the features of the new and old annuities. And you (or your child) should plan on conducting a thorough investigation of the new contract before making the switch.

6. Deterrent to Early Withdrawal The IRS imposes a 10% penalty on any gains withdrawn from an annuity before the annuitant turns 59½ (this is a trade-off for receiving tax-deferral on all capital gains and income). But this 10% penalty can actually work in your favor if you're trying to teach your child to defer gratification and keep the money designated toward her retirement goals.

Say you put $5,000 into a variable annuity for your child when she was five years old, and she becomes the owner when she reaches adulthood (18 or 21, depending on your state). The account grows at a 10% annual rate of return, until it reaches about $87,000 by the time she turns 35. At that time, she decides she needs a new car, and is lusting after the elegant and expensive Lexus/Mercedes/BMW touring sedan (remember when a car could be a status symbol just by having "rich, Corinthian leather"?). She's taken the test drive, and although her current income doesn't justify buying the car, and you told her the account was designed to supplement her retirement, she decides to tap into the nest egg you established.

If the money is in an index mutual fund or common stocks, the only thing keeping her from withdrawing it is the tax on long-term capital gains, which may be anywhere from 10% to 20% of the unrealized profits.

But if her only source of funds is from an annuity, after calculating the cost of withdrawing the money, the final amount looks something like this:

Annuity value	$87,000
Initial deposit (no taxes or penalty on this)	−5,000
Amount subject to tax and penalty	$82,000
Federal and state taxation @35%	−28,700
10% early withdrawal penalty	−8,200
Amount left over	$45,100
Plus initial deposit	5,000
Total net amount	$50,100

By withdrawing the money before retirement, your child has cost herself $36,900—over 40% of the value. And if she were to keep the money in the account, under the same circumstances it would be worth millions at her retirement, while the luxury car will have become a rusting piece of junk.

Now she still may choose to bite the bullet and pay the taxes and penalties, but if she has even an ounce of common sense, she will rethink the idea of withdrawing the money from the annuity, and perhaps consider a more moderately priced car.

And an added bonus for you is that the taxes and penalties are imposed by the government, not you! Uncle Sam is the big, mean bully keeping your child from detouring off the road to financial security. When she complains to you, you can shrug your shoulders and act as if you feel just as bad as she does.

7. Guaranteed Death Benefit Most modern variable annuities have some form of assurance that your child's beneficiaries will receive a guaranteed amount if the child passes away, regardless of the account's investment performance. The amount can range from just the initial deposit amount, to the highest value of the account on any previous contract anniversary, regardless of what the actual amount is at the time of death.

When I would tell people about this feature during the stock market boom of the 1990s, they would usually started nodding off or checking their watches. But then the Great Tech Stock Meltdown of 2000 came, and all of a sudden people were reminded that stocks can, and do, go down. And sometimes they stay down for a long time. The Dow Jones Industrial Average first hit 1,000 in 1968, and it didn't hit 2,000 for almost twenty years after that.

Knock on wood, we won't go through the misery of the 1970s again (although I'm hearing more disco music today than I have in a long time—will women soon be sporting Dorothy Hamill hairstyles again?). But if we do, the beneficiaries of annuities with a guaranteed minimum death benefit will be better off than those without.

8. Doesn't Hurt College Financial Aid Eligibility Because variable annuities are looked upon as retirement savings accounts, most college financial aid offices do not consider them as an eligible source of funds to pay for college. Consequently, your 18-year-old child might have tens of thousand of dollars in her name in a variable annuity, and still qualify for loans and scholarships that would have been unavailable if the money were in mutual funds or stocks outside of the annuity.

This doesn't mean that you can't use the proceeds of a variable annuity to pay for your child's college education. But if you do, remember you will have to pay income taxes and penalties on the previous gains made in the account. Let's say when your child was born you deposited $5,000 into a variable annuity. After eighteen years of 10% annual rate of return the account is worth about $28,000. If this account is the difference between her going to college and going to work in a coal mine, this is what your net amount would be:

Annuity value	$28,000
Original deposit	−5,000
Amount subject to tax and penalty	$23,000
Federal and state tax @ 25%	−5,750
10% early withdrawal penalty	−2,300
Amount left over	$14,950
Plus original deposit	5,000
Total	$19,950

Under this scenario, withdrawing the money to pay college expenses will cost over $8,000 in taxes and penalties—about 29% of the original amount. Plus, your child will no longer be able to watch that money grow toward a million dollars in future years. But in some cases the trade-off is worth it, especially if the account is used as a last resort.

Some insurance and investment advisers may tell you that variable annuities are a

suitable savings vehicle for a child's college education. They might mean well, but in most cases mutual funds outside of an annuity are a much better
choice for this purpose. Better yet, use the QSTP discussed in Chapter 2.

---

9. Multiple Payout Options. Your child can withdraw money
from the variable annuity in several different ways, depending
on which makes the most sense for her needs and situation:

Lump sum: The easiest method, but one that also results in
the highest level of taxation.

Annuitization: This feature allows the money to be paid to
your child in increments over a number of years, or even as
income guaranteed for life (or for your child's lifetime and
the life of your child's spouse, for example). Choosing this
method allows the child to waive the 10% early withdrawal
penalty, even if she is under the age of 59½ when the payments begin. But once the payment stream has begun, it
usually cannot be stopped or changed for any reason.

10. Protection from Creditors Under the laws of some states,
annuities cannot be "attached" by creditors if the owner has filed
for bankruptcy protection. This means if your child runs into financial trouble, she can still have an income stream from which
to draw support. A competent tax attorney can tell you how annuities may be treated for this purpose in your child's state.

Disadvantages of a Variable Annuity

1. Higher Commissions and Fees As you can see, annuities
have many benefits. But you pay for those benefits in the form
of higher sales charges and expenses than most other types of
stock, bond, or mutual fund investments.

Although investors typically don't pay an initial sales
charge to purchase an annuity, that doesn't mean the stockbro-

ker or insurance agent is helping you for free. The adviser gets paid up to 7% of the initial deposit amount of an annuity. The insurance company then deducts fees (as part of the "mortality and expense" charge) from the annuity account to make up the payment the insurance company has made to the adviser. This extra fee is usually around 1.0% to 1.5% annually, and comes out of the return of the account. This means if the variable account makes 10% in a given year, the net return to the investor may be 8.5% to 9.0%.

Keep in mind that there is a mutual fund inside the variable annuity "jar," and that fund also has expenses. These costs usually run between 0.5% to 1.5% per year. And finally, most insurance companies charge an annual "contract fee" that is between $25 and $35, although this fee is often waived for accounts over $50,000 in value.

Even though you never get a bill for most of these charges, they are deducted from annuity account values, and as such you need to be aware of them. If your child accumulates a million dollars in a variable annuity and the annual expenses total 3%, she is spending $30,000 per year for the management of the funds and the benefit of tax deferral. If you are paying an extra annual fee of 1% (versus that of a mutual fund) on a $5,000 deposit into a variable annuity, the difference might look like this after sixty-five years:

	Hypothetical Annual Rates of Return	
	9%	**10%**
$5,000 deposit after sixty-five years	$1,354,229	$2,451,853

A difference of almost $1.1 million! To be fair to the insurance companies, you may make up a large portion of that difference in the extra taxes you would be paying over the years, as was shown in the chart on page 116.

My guess is that although your 65-year-old child will be

thankful for any investment you make on her behalf, she would appreciate your having the foresight to examine the expenses of a particular variable annuity to make sure you are saving as much in costs as possible.

If you are a "do-it-yourselfer" you will be happy to know that some companies are bringing the "no-load" concept to variable annuities. These stripped-down accounts are sold directly to the investor (little or no help means you pay little or no commission), and sometimes have fewer bells and whistles than traditional adviser-sold annuities. Consequently, the annual expenses are lower.

2. Taxation Issues Some of the attraction of a variable annuity is the very fact that all taxes are avoided until the funds are withdrawn. The benefits are that the earnings in the account are reinvested and compounded, rather than having to use withdrawals to pay taxes each year. Since there are no taxes to declare, there is also no annual 1099 form generated by the investment, thus there is less paperwork.

But remember that when they are withdrawn, all earnings of an annuity are taxed as ordinary income, rather than broken down between income and capital gains. If you were to choose a mutual fund for your child rather than an annuity, a good-sized portion of the appreciation would be capital gains, and the long-term component of the capital gains would be taxed at a lower rate than the earnings withdrawn from an annuity.

And some recent changes in the tax code have lowered capital gains tax rates, while maintaining or even raising income tax rates. If the tax code gives us future moves in this direction, it will make annuities even less attractive than tax-efficient mutual funds or ownership of individual stocks, at least from a tax standpoint.

3. The 10% Penalty The IRS treats annuities as retirement planning vehicles, and therefore allows the income and capital gains to accumulate with no taxation until withdrawal. The downside to this is if your child makes any withdrawals before turning 59½, the IRS imposes an extra 10% penalty on any withdrawals of income or gains from the account, on top of the income taxes! However, the 10% penalty can be avoided in the following situations:

- Annuitization (equal payments over the annuitant's life expectancy)
- Death benefit paid to a beneficiary under 59½
- Withdrawals based on a 72(t) plan (a CPA, financial adviser, or the insurance company has information on this loophole)

Getting Started

The Securities and Exchange Commission has published a thorough look at the opportunities and pitfalls of using annuities, and it is free of charge to any interested investor. Go to www.sec.gov/investor/pubs/varannty.htm.

In your search for a variable annuity, you should look for a product that has the following criteria:

- Low annual expenses
- Little or no annual contract fee
- Wide range of reputable investment options
- A minimum initial investment that meets your needs

Although the vast majority of variable annuities are sold through advisers (and therefore have sales charges), there is a growing number of companies that offer no-load or low-load annuities to do-it-yourself investors:

Company	Web Site
Fidelity	www.fidelity.com
TIAA-CREF	www.tiaa-cref.org
Vanguard	www.vanguard.com
Schwab	www.schwab.com
BRKDirect	www.brkdirect.com

When you are gathering information on their variable annuity offerings, inform them of your desired deposit amount to make sure it meets the minimum deposit requirements. If you are purchasing an annuity on your own, make sure you choose one that has little or no redemption charge (remember, you are not going to get very much help, so you shouldn't have to pay a lot in the form of sales charges).

If you want your child to become the owner of the account when she reaches adulthood, you should set up the account as follows:

Owner: (Custodian Name) for (Child's Name) under UTMA
Annuitant: Child
Beneficiary: Child's estate (or a person)

Initial Deposit Needed to Make a Kid a Millionaire at Age 65

Assuming a 10% net annualized rate of return

Child's Age	Deposit
Newborn	$ 2,040
5	3,285
10	5,289
15	8,518
20	13,719
25	22,095
30	35,584
35	57,309
40	92,296

Tangible proof of "Ten Things You Need to Know," #1 and #2 (see pages 38 and 39). For the cost of a week's vacation, you can develop the foundation of a retirement plan that could serve your young child for decades.

chapter five

Your Comfortable Retirement, Your Millionaire Kid, and Nothing for Uncle Sam

Your Roth IRA Is a Gift from the Government

Most of the trillions of dollars that Americans have invested are focused toward two goals: a comfortable retirement and providing for children.

But how in the world do you address both goals at the same time? Many of my clients call me up and say, "We've got a few extra dollars to invest. Should we put it toward our retirement, or should we do something for the kids?"

I say, "Yes."

There is a financial vehicle that can pull "double duty" to help you meet your family's financial aspirations. It allows you to put money aside today in your choice of stocks, bonds, or mutual funds, and watch it grow tax-deferred until your retirement. And then you can pull it out tax-free to support your lifestyle or give it to your child. In addition, you can use this account as a way to:

- Prevent the government's forcing you to begin liquidating your retirement account at age 70½.

- Transfer money to your child immediately at your death, avoiding probate
- Help pay for a child's college education
- Generate millions of dollars of income to your children, at the same time avoiding the reach of the IRS

The option is called the Roth IRA, and it first became available to investors in 1998. The account is similar to a regular IRA, with a few twists. You don't get a tax deduction on current contributions, but with the exception of a very few limitations, you don't have to pay any federal taxes on the gains when you withdraw your money.

You probably have heard about it, but if you are like most Americans you haven't taken advantage of it yet (although the Investment Company Institute says that as of June 2000, almost 10 million American households contained a Roth IRA owner).

This account is one of the greatest gifts the government has ever given investors, and it can be a powerful tool to help yourself and your child.

Getting Money into a Roth IRA

There are two ways for you to accumulate money in a Roth IRA. You can make annual contributions, or you can convert an existing IRA into a Roth IRA. Both methods are subject to limitations based on your adjusted gross income (AGI).

Contributing

You can contribute up to $2,000 to a Roth IRA for the 2001 tax year (as long as you have earnings of at least that amount), and that number rises to $3,000 for 2002. And people age 50 and over can contribute $500 over the annual limit for 2002 to 2005, and $1,000 over after 2005.

Under the current law, the annual limit will keep rising until

2008, when the maximum reaches $5,000. And there is supposed to be a Roth 401(k) plan we can begin using in 2006, but don't count on it.

In addition, a Roth IRA can be established by a spouse who doesn't work outside the home (and doesn't earn any income), as long as the total contributions don't exceed the *working* spouse's earnings, and don't go over the annual limit. For example, if you earned at least $4,000, you can make a $2,000 Roth IRA contribution for yourself, and another $2,000 Roth IRA contribution for your stay-at-home spouse (depending on your viewpoint, this is either a great stride forward for recognizing the economic value of a stay-at-home parent, or it is one more good loophole to shelter as much income as possible from the voracious IRS).

Putting $4,000 per year into a Roth IRA can have a tremendous outcome for your family. If a married couple contributes $2,000 each (about five dollars a day) into a Roth IRA for thirty-five years, and the funds earn a 10% annual rate of return, the accounts would be worth $1,084,097! And as long as the Roth IRA owners are over 59½ they can withdraw that money and pay no federal taxes. Assuming the withdrawals would otherwise be taxed at 35%, they would need almost $1.7 million in a regular IRA, 401(k) plan, or tax-deferred annuity to get the same after-tax dollar amount.

If this isn't enough of a motivation for you to begin contributing, keep in mind there is an income limitation for making Roth IRA contributions. Your maximum contribution amount is gradually reduced as your income approaches the following levels for each filing status in 2001:

Filing Status	Income Phaseouts
Married filing jointly	**$150,000–$160,000**
Single	**$90,000–$110,000**

And if you earned more than $160,000 (joint filer) or $110,000 (single) in 2001, you are flatly prohibited from contributing to a Roth IRA (but you can contribute for your child, if he has earned income—see Chapter 8). Even though you might qualify now, you might make too much money in the coming years, preventing you from making contributions (I know, it's a good problem to have). You'll kick yourself for not putting money into the Roth IRA when you had the chance.

If your income falls under the maximum, you can make an annual Roth IRA contribution even if you are already putting money into a company-sponsored retirement plan, such as a 401(k). And although you can split contributions between a Roth IRA and a regular IRA, you should never put money into a nondeductible regular IRA if you have an opportunity to use the Roth. Doing so is like putting a note on your tax return telling the IRS to "Please keep any refund I might have coming, and spend it the way you see fit."

Advantages of a Roth IRA

1. No Taxes, Yet No Loss of Control You want to provide for the financial independence of your child, both for his benefit and for the tax break on earnings. But you are hesitant to put the money in your child's name for one or more of the following reasons:

- You are concerned the child might not be mature enough to handle the money wisely when he turns 18
- You are worried you might need the money for your retirement
- You don't want to jeopardize his eligibility for any financial aid packages if he goes to college.

Putting money into a Roth IRA solves all these problems. You keep control over the assets, yet the earnings in the account will not be taxable to you. And because the money is in a retirement account in your name, the value of the account will not affect your child's financial aid eligibility.

2. No Mandatory Distribution Liquidation (and taxation) of your regular IRA must begin in the year you turn 70½. But your Roth IRA can remain untouched as long as you live, and can be passed intact to your heirs (see page 137, "Taking Money Out of a Roth IRA").

Disadvantages of a Roth IRA

1. No Tax Deduction Unlike a regular IRA, you put after-tax dollars into a Roth IRA. This means that contributing to a Roth IRA instead of a regular IRA can raise your annual tax bill by as much as a few hundred dollars each year, although the income limits make deductibility of a regular IRA contribution difficult to reach for many investors (especially if they also qualify for a retirement plan at work).

2. The Money Is Tied Up Unless it is for certain circumstances you cannot gain access to the funds before turning 59½. Pulling the money out before this date will mean you pay taxes on the earnings, plus a 10% penalty.

Converting an IRA to a Roth IRA

If you have an existing IRA, you may be able to convert part or all of your existing regular IRA to a Roth, as long as you have less than $100,000 in annual adjusted gross income. If you do choose to convert, you must pay taxes on the value of the IRA, in the year of conversion. The assets converted are added to your adjusted gross income, and taxed just as if you'd earned them. But for a small amount of tax pain today, you and your child can enjoy a large amount of financial gain tomorrow.

When does a conversion make sense? Well, from a tax standpoint, it is a good idea if the following are true:

• You expect to be in the same or higher tax bracket
  when you retire versus when you convert

- You have other retirement accounts, such as a 401(k), that you have no ability to convert
- You have enough liquid assets outside of the IRA to pay the taxes

You don't have to convert the entire amount of your IRA; as a matter of fact, you should usually only convert enough to keep you in the federal tax bracket of 27% (about $110,000 for married couples filing jointly in 2002). You can find the current tax brackets at www.irs.gov.

Advantages of Converting Your IRA to a Roth IRA

1. More Money at Retirement Even if you are only in a 28% tax bracket at retirement, you would need $1,388,888 in a regular IRA to equal $1 million in a Roth IRA. And because of the progressive increase in tax brackets, if you retired today and withdrew your money in a lump sum, you would need to withdraw over $1.6 million from your IRA to equal a $1 million lump sum withdrawal from a Roth IRA!

2. Tax Flexibility Say you have an IRA you are considering converting to a Roth, and you are also participating in your employer's 401(k). If you qualify, it would be highly beneficial for you to convert the IRA into a Roth. The combination of the two can significantly reduce your tax bill as you draw money from these accounts to support your retirement.

Why? Let's say you have $30,000 in your IRA now. You visit my office for advice. I recommend you convert it into a Roth IRA, and tell you that doing so will cost you about $8,000 in taxes this year. Your face turns pale, sweat beads on your forehead, and you become slightly nauseous. You stumble out of my office, mumbling something about, "He said he was going to *cut* our tax bill!"

Fast-forward thirty years from now. You are retiring, and your IRA that you neglected to convert has now grown to $500,000. You also have $500,000 in an IRA you have just rolled over from your employer's 401(k). The accounts earn 10% per year. You need $120,000 to live on after taxes (at 3% inflation, this buys you about $50,000 worth of goods in today's dollars). Assuming the current income tax brackets are raised 3% each year, your withdrawals would be taxed at 15% up to about $109,000, and 27% after that. The funds would last as follows:

IRA amount	$1,000,000
Annual growth rate	10%
Annual after-tax withdrawal	$120,000
Years to depletion	**12 years**

I bet you thought that even in thirty years a million-dollar IRA would give you more than enough to retire. And it might, especially since you may be fortunate enough to be able to rely on some Social Security payments (although I sure wouldn't count on it). But between taxes and inflation, you might have less money to retire on than you thought.

Now let's say, upon my advice, you converted the IRA to a Roth IRA. It is now worth $500,000, and you still have $500,000 in an IRA you rolled over from an employer's 401(k). We'll use the same retirement age and return rate as the first example. Only this time you make annual withdrawals from the regular IRA just to reach the top of the 15% federal tax bracket (in 2001 it was $45,200 for married, filing jointly). The rest of the money you need to reach your $120,000 after-tax annual amount will come out of the Roth IRA. After the IRA is depleted, you can withdraw all the money you need from your Roth IRA. How long would it last?

IRA amount	$500,000
Roth IRA amount	$500,000
Annual growth rate	10%
Annual after-tax withdrawal amount (with enough taken from the regular IRA to reach the top of the 15% tax	

bracket and the rest coming from the Roth
IRA. After the IRA is depleted, the money
comes solely from the Roth IRA) $120,000
Years to depletion   **15.5 years**

By converting your IRA to a Roth IRA, you've bought an extra 3½ years of comfortable retirement in exchange for a long-forgotten $8,000 payment to the IRS. (I know what you're thinking . . . "What about the future value of the $8,000?"—at 10%, it is worth about $140,000, or less than one year's pre-tax living expenses.) It seems well worth it to me, but you should make your decision based on your circumstances.

3. No Mandatory Distribution A regular IRA requires you to begin making withdrawals at the age of 70½, at a schedule the IRS hopes depletes the account over the lifetime of you and your beneficiary (the IRS wants the money withdrawn so they can tax it on the way out). The Roth IRA, however, requires only that the money be withdrawn over the estimated lifetime of your oldest beneficiary, and even that only begins after your death. This means your Roth IRA can generate income to heirs for decades, and they won't have to pay taxes on the distributions (see page 138, "The 'Stretch' Roth IRA").

4. Reduction in Estate Taxes Any taxes you pay on a conversion from an IRA to a Roth IRA are immediately taken out of your estate, which may reduce the taxes your heirs will pay when you die.

Disadvantages of Converting Your IRA to a Roth IRA
1. The Big Tax Payment You might not have enough money set aside to make the extra tax payment. If you have already put that kind of money in a readily accessible fund, I would guess you probably aren't too excited about writing a check to the IRS (even though you were eventually going to pay taxes on the distribution, anyway).

So what are your other options? You can take extra money out of the IRA to pay the taxes, but this withdrawal only generates more tax liability, plus a 10% penalty if you are under 59½. Also, the large margin between the after-tax proceeds of the regular IRA versus the Roth IRA shrinks dramatically. If this is the only way you can afford to pay the taxes, I would forget about converting.

You could borrow the money to pay the taxes, but you would have to weigh the interest costs (and the risk of incurring more debt) against the potential benefits of the Roth. I am not a huge proponent of borrowing money to pay the tax on a conversion. But since it is possible to save hundreds of thousands of tax dollars down the road, obtaining a loan for a few thousand dollars might make sense, whether you use a straight consumer loan or borrow against your home equity.

2. Uncertainty of Tax Bracket During Retirement You can predict with some degree of certainty what your income tax bracket will be when you retire. But say you convert your regular IRA to a Roth, and the conversion is taxed at 36%. Then for some reason you are in the 15% bracket in retirement. The benefits to converting diminish substantially, and in many cases it would be much more advantageous to not convert. However, converting to a Roth may still be a good idea, especially if you are concerned about the issue of taxation for your IRA beneficiaries.

After hearing the reasons to convert a regular IRA to a Roth IRA, some people say, "I'm not worried about my tax bracket being higher. I just don't trust the federal government to keep their hands off Roth IRA withdrawals." Indeed, you don't need to be a member of your local militia to view the actions of the U.S. Treasury with a cynical eye. And going through the conversion is really a trade-off: you are paying taxes now, to avoid paying in the future.

But in just the first two years of availability, over 10 million Americans had either opened a Roth IRA or converted their regular IRA into a Roth. I would call this a pretty powerful voting bloc, and one that will only continue to grow in size and influence in the future. Politicians do a lot of stupid things, but most of them are savvy enough to avoid reneging on a promise to millions of voters with billions of dollars at stake. Have faith that Uncle Sam will stick to the original agreement.

3. Five-Year Rule You can't withdraw money from a converted Roth IRA until five years after the conversion date. If you are approaching retirement and will need money from your IRA for living expenses in the next five years, leave a sufficient amount in the account.

Don't convert an IRA to a Roth IRA if you expect to be applying for financial aid for your child's college expenses in the next few years. The resulting rise in your adjusted gross income (remember, the converted amount is added to your AGI) can drastically raise your family's expected contribution, thereby reducing the size of your aid package.

Taking Money Out of a Roth IRA

Envision yourself in your sixties. You and your Roth IRA have made it to retirement. Now comes the fun part. For every dollar other investors are withdrawing from their IRAs, they might be sending 30 to 50 cents to the IRS. You, on the other hand, will be pulling out only what you need, with no regard for the government whatsoever. And if you don't need the money for your own expenses, your children and grandchildren will be the beneficiaries of a lifelong stream of tax-free income.

Money for You

If you need the money to support your lifestyle, go ahead and dip into the account. As long as you are over 59½ and five years have gone by since any conversion, there are no taxes or penalties. You don't even need to be retired to get at the money. You can still be working but use the Roth IRA as a tax-free way to supplement your earnings.

But the longer you can delay the withdrawals, the better the value. If you have a $100,000 Roth IRA at age 60, letting it grow for another fifteen years at 10% will give you over $400,000 to spend on that condo in Costa Rica.

Money for Your Child

After you turn 59½: By the time you reach this age, two things will likely have occurred. You will have a better idea of how much (if any) money you will need to take from your Roth IRA to support yourself. And if you decide you can afford to help your child, you will also have a pretty good idea if he is going to handle the money in a responsible manner.

You (and your spouse) can start gifting the money to him at a rate of $10,000 each per year, for a total of $20,000 per child, and still avoid incurring the gift tax. In addition, you can also give $20,000 to his spouse, his children, or anyone else you please.

After you're gone—The "stretch" Roth IRA: If you are ready to give up control of your Roth IRA only after they pry your cold, lifeless fingers off the monthly statements, your child will have a few choices as to how quickly he withdraws funds from the account. If he needs the money right away, he can take it all out, again with no federal taxes.

But a smart child (like yours) will not do that. Instead, he will take the money out only as fast as the IRS requires, creating a "stretch" Roth IRA for himself. According to the law, he must take out a minimal amount each year, based on his life expectancy (although this amount is determined by a number of factors, it might be as little as 5% to 10% of the value in the early years). But he can leave the rest of the money to accumulate tax-free.

You shouldn't dismiss this feature of your Roth IRA. We don't know what the future laws will be, and what changes will come that might affect this scenario. But if today's rules apply, one year's contribution can mean several decades of annual five-figure checks sent to your child, with no federal taxation.

If you put just $2,000 into a Roth today, and you "journey to the great beyond" fifty years from now, that deposit will then be worth almost $235,000, assuming a 10% annual return. If your child inherits the account and has a thirty-year life expectancy at the time, he will have to withdraw only about $9,300 in the first year. And over the thirty or so years during his withdrawal period, he would receive checks totaling well over a million dollars.

A Roth IRA left to your next generation is an extremely valuable asset. But when left to your grandchildren, the wealth-generating effect borders on the miraculous. Their longer life expectancy could allow *tens of millions* of dollars to accumulate, with no federal taxation! See Chapter 13 for more information.

Combining a Roth IRA with a Trust What if you are worried that after you're gone your child will immediately spend the entire Roth IRA? Then you will be happy to know that with some assistance from a qualified attorney, you can not only provide for yourself and your child but also:

- Create a "wealth factory," generating tax-free growth for decades
- Prevent incompetent or immature heirs from squandering your gift

- Tailor your bequests to the unique situation of each one of your beneficiaries

The powerful solution lies in taking the advantages of the Roth one step further. As was noted before, upon your death the beneficiary of your Roth IRA can take the money out immediately, take minimum required distributions based on his life expectancy, or withdraw the funds at a rate in between these two extremes.

But what if you don't want your child to have the option to take the money out immediately? For attorney fees of a few hundred to a few thousand dollars, you can create a trust that, upon your death, begins to receive the required distributions from your Roth IRA. You then have the assets from the trust made available to your child, but only in the circumstances you establish when you write the trust agreement. The setup looks like this:

The trust is not the owner of your Roth IRA, just the beneficiary (there is a difference, in the eyes of the IRS). The amount funneled from the Roth IRA to the trust equals the IRS-required minimum distribution, based on the life expectancy of the oldest beneficiary of the trust.

Advantage of Combining a Roth IRA with a Trust

Keeping the "Golden Eggs" Coming I can't emphasize strongly enough how potent an investment tool the Roth IRA is. There is virtually no other investment vehicle that is as flexible, available, and convenient, and that offers the potential for growth over the long term without incurring federal taxation!

Yet your heirs may not realize just how fortunate they are to own a Roth, especially one that may be worth hundreds of thousands of dollars. Your child or grandchild may be tempted by that large tax-free pool of money, and spend it before he realizes what he has done. Like the childhood fable, he may be tempted to kill the goose (enjoying a nice dinner, but never being able to have any more golden eggs).

The trust helps prevent this from happening. You can write the language of the trust so that he receives all income from the investments within. These can be stocks, bonds, certificates of deposit, or any other type of liquid investment. (The trustee you appoint decides which types of financial vehicles are the most prudent.) If you want the trust to grow and generate as little income as possible, you should specify that the trustee choose common stocks paying little or no dividends. If you want the child to receive a greater income, the trustee should put a larger portion of the assets in bonds, or stocks with higher dividends.

You accomplish two goals by having him take the income from the assets in the trust, and only the trust:

- You give him some money, but hopefully not more than he can handle
- You help him avoid the high tax rates on money left in trusts (in 2001, almost 40% on any earnings over $8,900 not distributed to the beneficiary)

Protecting your child's nest egg from your child doesn't mean you have to deprive him, or that the trust can't help him in emergencies. You are free to write in the trust that he can dip into principal to pay for college, a new house, or whatever else you feel is justified. And since eventually you probably want him to have control over the money, in most states you can allow him to become the trustee at a certain age (say, 30 or 35). By then he may have reached a level of maturity that allows him to use the money in the wise way you intended. The issues and details of establishing a trust for your beneficiaries are covered in Chapter 12.

You can split your Roth IRA into as many accounts as you want. Then you can create an account (and trust) for each child or grandchild whom you wish to help, and the withdrawal schedule on each child's portion of the inherited Roth will be based on his life expectancy.

Disadvantages of Combining a Roth IRA with a Trust

1. Congress May Close the Window This is such an effective weapon against taxation that some consultants believe Congress may eventually disallow this maneuver, or at least make it less advantageous to pursue it. Although it is difficult to predict when or even if this will happen, you may be "grandfathered" if you take action before any attempts are made to restrict the use of a Roth IRA and a trust.

2. Expenses Creating the second layer of protection between your child and her money will increase the administration and legal costs. Therefore, it is only advisable to establish a trust if the Roth IRA will have a large balance, or you are especially worried about your child's ability to handle the money.

College Factor

There are two ways you can use a Roth IRA to help pay for your child's college education. First of all, if you expect to be over the age of 59½ when your child enters college, saving money in a Roth IRA allows you to avoid federal taxation on earnings and withdrawals, without putting the money in your child's name. Once your child needs the money, you can simply withdraw the funds, tax-free and with no penalty, and help him with college expenses.

If your child will need help with college costs before you turn 59½, you can still tap into a portion of your Roth IRA. Simply designate the withdrawals as being your *contributions*, and you will pay no taxes or penalties on the amount. Keep in mind, however, that once you withdraw this money it will not earn you any more tax-free gains and interest, so make sure you first exhaust all of your other options.

Getting Started

I don't think it's possible to oversave for retirement, and I know nobody enjoys paying any more taxes than they have to. You can analyze the best way to use the Roth IRA in the following steps:

Contributing

1. Can you afford to make a Roth IRA contribution?
2. Do you (or your spouse) have earned income?
3. Is your income below the limit?

Converting

1. Do you have an IRA to convert?
2. Are you under the income limit?
3. Upon withdrawal, do you think your tax bracket will be less than or equal to what it is when you convert?
4. Do you have money to pay the taxes at conversion?

With either contributing or converting, you also need to decide if you want the money to be left directly to your heirs or if you want a trust to "catch" the distributions first.

Resources

Most mutual fund and investment advisory firms have literature and Web sites covering the Roth IRA, and many of them also have calculators you can use to see how valuable the Roth IRA might be to you.

There is an abundance of articles on the Roth IRA at www.rothira.com. Some of the information is written for advisers, but other items will be useful to you, even if you are just starting to research the subject.

Finally, if you are suffering from insomnia and are interested in learning more about the tax implications of the Roth IRA, you may want to kill two birds with one stone by consulting IRS Publication 590, *Individual Retirement Arrangements*.

chapter six

To Have and to Hold: The Low Cost, Low Maintenance, and Big Potential of Common Stocks

Many of the Secure clients I work with have a particular type of investment that they treat like a cherished member of their families. The object of their affection is a holding of several thousand shares of common stock in a publicly traded company. In general, these "beloved relatives" have the following characteristics:

- The stock is from a decades-old "blue-chip" company, based in the United States
- The shares were first purchased many years ago, and may even have been passed down from a previous generation
- The shares have split many times
- The original purchase price is a tiny fraction of the current price, often pennies on the dollar
- The shares repay the holder's original investment back *each year* in the form of dividends

The shareholders don't worry about price fluctuations or market crashes because they know that if the price of the stock does fall, chances are it will likely rise again. And it's not going back to what they originally paid for it. As a matter of fact, the only worry these people have is that their company might be bought out for cash, and then they would have a substantial capital gains liability on their hands (but the huge windfall will pay any tax bill many times over).

These people have been well rewarded for their Secure behavior. They didn't panic during the awful markets of the 1970s, or the various October crashes of the late 1980s and 1990s.

When I met these people during my early years as a financial adviser, I would express my admiration to these shareholders for the large position they had accumulated.

But then my broker "training" would kick in and I just had to give them a lecture on the virtues of diversification. I seem to recall frequently using the phrase "all of your eggs in one basket." I told them how their company's share price might have underperformed other investments during a particular time period, and that the assets could have been better invested somewhere else. There are many "leading" companies that are no more. I would go on and on, until I realized they weren't really listening to me anymore.

Haranguing a long-term holder of a blue-chip stock about the need to spread his assets around is like advising him to sell his children at public auction. Most people politely declined my advice to diversify. But one candid gentleman with a huge number of shares of Microsoft enlightened me. "Lack of diversification hasn't hurt Bill Gates any!" he said.

Good point.

• • •

Although most common stock mutual funds own hundreds of different companies, when speaking off the record many fund managers will admit they would rather own just a few companies, representing the managers' best ideas.

Before long I changed my philosophy slightly, and although I still believe in the benefits of diversification, I am willing to acknowledge the value of "putting all your eggs in one basket, and keeping an eye on 'em!"

You may have heard stories like this yourself. Somebody

bought so-and-so blue-chip stock, never did anything with it, and years later now has over a million dollars in the company. Part of the reason you might be especially attracted to using this method of providing long-term financial security for your child is that you rarely hear about the *opposite* outcome. It doesn't have a lot of compelling narrative value ("Did you know that Uncle Charlie put $500 into Zippy Oil in 1952, and two years later it went out of business?").

Although building serious wealth through long-term ownership of common stocks doesn't happen often enough, *it really does happen.* Not every common stock price rises over the long term, yet thousands of people have made billions of dollars over the last few decades by simply buying stock in a good company and never selling it.

Common stock ownership can be a great way for anyone to make a kid a millionaire. This method has the following features:

- Low initial investment (a few hundred dollars)
- Low taxes
- Low commission expenses
- Natural path to teaching your child about business, money, and investing

You don't need thousands of dollars to begin accumulating wealth this way. You don't even need to use a broker to get started (unless you want her to recommend a stock for you). But you do need to start. And your first step is to pick the companies that you are going to love.

Finding the Right Stock

How should you pick a stock for your child? First of all, it is easier to tell you how people *don't* accumulate sizable wealth by owning shares in common stocks:

1. They buy obscure penny stocks in some kind of mining company or crazy technology stock,

usually reassuring themselves by saying, "How much lower can it go?"

2. They buy stocks with money they can't afford to put aside
3. They buy stocks based on rumors, or short-term news stories
4. They worry about the stock's day-to-day price fluctuations
5. They get upset if there is another stock that has risen more than theirs has
6. If the stock they buy goes up a little right after they purchase it, they sell it
7. If the stock goes down a little right after they purchase it, they sell it

---

A common mistake people make when they are buying shares of stock is to think that if they have $1,000 to invest, it is better to buy 1,000 shares of a $1 stock, than it is to have 100 shares of a $10 stock. This is a pet peeve of mine. The $1 stock is cheap for a reason. There are no well-run, profitable companies with a great long-term outlook that trade for $1. As a matter of fact, not only will fewer shares of a $10 stock likely do better than more shares of a $1 stock but I'm inclined to believe 20 shares of a $50 stock are more likely to make you and your child money over the long run than more shares of a cheaper-priced stock.

You don't need to be a CPA or a CEO to be a successful long-term owner of stocks. But you do need to have a basic under-standing of the company's business so you don't get frightened out of ownership during bad times (and there will be bad times). You need to know how they make money, who their customers and competitors are, and what their long-term strategy is. By "adopting" these shares, you and your child are more likely to stick with this one through good times and bad to get a chance at spectacular long-term growth.

1. Buy What You Know The good news for you and your child is that there are many people with million-dollar holdings in a single stock. Very few of them made their original purchase based on hours of research, inside information, or any astute knowledge of an arcane industry. Instead, they bought the stock because they worked for the company, lived near the headquarters, or bought the products the company made.

Whether they knew it or not, these people were following the advice of Peter Lynch, the legendary mutual fund manager who used to run the Fidelity Magellan fund. He is a proponent of investing in what you know, whether it's a store you patronize, a company based in your area, or perhaps one a friend or relative works for.

Just because you are familiar with the company, this doesn't mean you can ignore the fundamentals, like earnings and sales growth. But starting with only companies you are connected to is a good way to use your eyes and ears, before you have to "run the numbers."

For example, hark with me back to my fifth birthday party. It was 1971, and a new McDonald's restaurant had recently opened up in our town. My parents took my friends and me to this new restaurant, and we had a great time. The place was shiny and clean. The lines at the counter were seven deep. The food was exactly as we expected—fast, hot, and *good* (especially to a bunch of kindergarteners).

Had my mom and dad read this chapter before my birthday party, they might have taken a look around at how much fun the kids were having, how reasonably priced the food was, and how we begged to go back at every opportunity. They might have decided to do some research on the company and try to be a part of its success. They might have called a broker and purchased $1,000 worth of McDonald's stock.

I should be so fortunate. My mother and father did a lot of wonderful things for me, but they never bought any McDonald's stock for me (though they did purchase thousands of dollars' worth of cheeseburgers for me over the next decade). But if they had bought the stock, their $1,000 investment would have returned *900%* over the next twenty-nine years, to a value of over $90,000 by the end of 1999.

2. Analyst Recommendations Research from the big Wall Street investment firms can be a good place to start. But keep in mind that analysts are paid to monitor short-term fluctuations in the companies they follow, and make recommendations based on what the price of a company's stock is likely to do over the next few weeks or months. An investment firm may put a "buy" recommendation on a company at $40 per share, with a price target of $50 for the coming year. If the firm is right, they might change their recommendation to "hold" or even "sell" once the price hits $50. The investors who followed the advice might make a 25% profit, and look for the firm's next idea.

But the best way for your child to become enriched through ownership of common stocks is for you (and her) to adopt a long-term perspective. Shareholders who have owned great companies for decades have held their stock through all kinds of upgrades and downgrades, and have never paid much attention to the short-term swings of the stock price. But analysts are judged on their picks over a matter of months or even *weeks*. Consequently, this type of research can provide some insight, but the long-term value of the information is relatively low.

3. Do-It-Yourself Research If you want to do it well, follow in the footsteps of the master. To learn to play golf, you'd watch Tiger Woods. For basketball, Michael Jordan would be good for you to emulate. For investing, where do you turn?

We could all do worse than match the long-term results of the "Oracle of Omaha," Warren Buffett. This self-deprecating septuagenarian has been investing in public and private companies for decades. He ranked fourth on the 2000 *Forbes 400* list of richest Americans, with an estimated net worth of about $28 billion. He missed out on the boom (but also the bust) of the Internet era, and when he is rumored to be establishing a position in a particular company, it is usually enough to boost the company's stock price by several dollars. People figure if Warren Buffett is buying it, so should they.

You can save yourself some time and align your child's interests with Buffett's by buying stock in the legendary investor's publicly traded company, Berkshire Hathaway. Investors in this conglomerate averaged about 25% annual return from 1986 to the end of 2000, compared to around 13% annual return in the Standard & Poor's 500 index over the same period (Warren Buffett would be the first one to tell you that his past performance is no indication of future results). You can learn more about the company and the businesses in which Buffet has invested at www.berkshirehathaway.com. This site also contains Buffet's witty and informative annual letters to his shareholders (I believe these should be required reading for all long-term owners of common stock).

If you would rather purchase shares in a company based on your own research, it may still pay to evaluate a company the way Buffett does: He cruises stock chat rooms on the Internet, looking for tips from anonymous people with user names like "ezmoney283."

I'm kidding.

He actually considers each company as if he were buying the entire business. It's the same way you would if your neighbor or relative came to you and asked if you wanted to plunk down some of your hard-earned money to buy a piece of the guy's tavern/restaurant/mini golf course. Buffett judges the company's financials, past and future, products, and management. If he thinks he will earn more by investing money in the company than by leaving it in cash (or another company), he commits to ownership, and rarely sells.

Where can you find a company's financial information on your own? Start with the Value Line reports, available at your local library. Or you can subscribe to the print or online edition at www.valueline.com. There are several other worthy sources, but none supplies so much financial information like earnings, amount of money borrowed, sales, etc., on one page of paper. And if you're really hungry for minute details, go to www.sec.gov, and search the *EDGAR* database of all the quarterly and annual reports every publicly traded company must file.

Once you get access to the information, though, you are going to need to know what to do with it. You might think you don't know the first thing about digesting all these numbers, but common sense can help you make your decision:

- *Sales*   Are they rising or falling?
- *Earnings*   Is the company making more profit each year? Can it keep it going into the future?
- *Debt*   Borrowing money is not necessarily bad, but too much debt (when compared to other companies in their industry) can be a red flag.
- *Dividends*   Does the company pay an annual dividend? Has it paid a dividend every year, and better yet, has it *raised* the dividend each year?

The Web site of The American Association of Individual Investors (www.aaii.com) provides tools to help you evaluate stocks according to several criteria, including one that estimates the benchmarks and factors used by Buffett.

---

4. Buy What Your Child Knows   Invest in companies whose products and services are part of your child's life. If your kid understands what the company does and can evaluate its products, she will, with a little encouragement from you and a quick explanation of how that company's health is contagious to her investment portfolio, soon be interested in the company itself.

I remember discussing Nike stock with some clients a few years ago. They were interested in purchasing shares, but as they were calling me to buy, their teenage son overheard our phone conversation and said, "Nikes suck. Nobody wears them anymore." They scolded him for his "coarse" assessment, but they also quizzed him about what he meant. He told them that at his school Nikes weren't cool, and most people were wearing boots of some kind or another. And when they did wear sneakers, they wore Vans.

The parents reconsidered, and ended up buying stock in the company that made Vans instead. It might have been just luck, but the last time I checked they had about twice as much money in the Vans stock as they would have had if they had purchased Nike. And their son reports to them regularly on how hot the new product line is, and what other products he and his friends are drooling over.

Some companies that might be a little more relevant to your kid's world include:

Company	Symbol
Campbell's Soup	CPB
Cedar Fair L.P. (amusement parks)	FUN
Coca-Cola	KO
Walt Disney	DIS
Hasbro	HAS
H. J. Heinz	HNZ
Hershey's	HSY
Home Depot	HD
Kellogg's	K
Mattel	MAT

(continued on next page)

Company	Symbol
McDonald's	MCD
Nike	NKE
Pepsi	PEP
Tricon Global (Pizza Hut, KFC, Taco Bell)	YUM
Topps	TOPP
Tootsie Roll	TR
Vans	VANS
Wal-Mart	WMT
W. J. Wrigley	WWY

You may want to point out to your child that even though she might technically be a part owner of say, Wendy's, she can't call the local restaurant up and demand they hire her best friend.

If your child has a strong interest in computers, you and she will have more than enough companies to pick from. I know one teenager who was sure Microsoft would one day dominate the computer software market, and asked his parents to consider buying the stock for him. They did some research and decided to follow his advice, putting in about $1,500 for him. That was in 1989; by the end of the 1990s, the young man's holdings in the company were worth about $180,000!

5. Spreading It Around What if you are investing for a child, and you *don't* pick the next Microsoft? What if you are like the people who put a thousand dollars into a great company like Minnesota Mining & Manufacturing (MMM) in 1973, only to see it "grow" to a little over $1,200 over the next *ten years* (and that's only if they reinvested the dividends)? Could you look your child in the eye and tell her your investment decision earned her around 2% annually over a ten-year period?

Me, neither. And to be fair to MMM, not many stocks went up very much over these years, and MMM went on to make spectacular returns for their shareholders the following decade.

Investing in just one company is a great way to make a lot of money over the long term, as long as you have the right company. If not, your child will be lucky to be a thousandaire, much less a millionaire. A possible Harvard education can turn into a chimney sweep degree from a correspondence school.

How can you improve your child's odds? One way is to diversify a little bit. Pick five stocks instead of just one, and hope that two will do about as well as the Standard & Poor's 500 index, one will do worse, and one may even go out of business. But you and your child might be fortunate enough to have a real "rocket ship" in your fifth stock. That rocket ship may be the key to giving your child financial independence.

Let's say you put $1,000 each into five different stocks for a five-year-old. After forty years, the five stocks have performed as follows:

Company #1	Went out of business
Company #2	Returned 5% annually
Company #3	Returned 10% annually
Company #4	Returned 10% annually
Company #5 (the rocket ship)	Returned 15% annually

How much money would this now-forty-five-year-old have?

Company #1	$ 0
Company #2	7,039
Company #3	45,259
Company #4	45,259
Company #5 (the rocket ship)	267,863
Total	$365,420

Five thousand dollars! That works out to an annual rate of return of 11.3% for the portfolio. If you doubt the likelihood of attaining a 15% return over forty years in one stock, you are right—that type of return is uncommon.

But then there is the story of a little discount store chain from Arkansas that went public in late 1970 (just a couple of years *before* a 40% loss in the Standard & Poor's 500 index). Despite widespread competition from established giants and newcomers alike, community resentment every time the company opened a new store, and even the death of its beloved founder, Wal-Mart rewarded the loyalty of its initial investors with an annual return of more than 35% through the end of 1999. Had you invested $500 for your child in 1970, her nest egg would have grown to over $3.5 million over those twenty-nine years, with hardly any taxes or commissions paid.

Making Your Purchase

Of course you can always start building your child's common stock portfolio by buying through a full-service or discount broker. But you can also purchase shares of stock in thousands of publicly traded companies via *direct stock purchase* (DSP) plans or *dividend reinvestment programs* (DRIPs).

DSPs allow you to purchase stock directly from the company, or to go through a clearinghouse. With either method there is usually a small fee charged (anywhere from $5 to $20 per transaction), and the minimum initial investment can be as little as $100, with $100 for subsequent investments. You can send in checks as you see fit, or in some cases set up a systematic withdrawal plan to buy shares on a regular basis. The funds can even be automatically deducted from your checking account.

Not all listed companies sell stock directly, and many clearinghouses offer only a limited number of available companies. If you're dying to buy shares in a particular company but can't purchase it through direct means, you will have to go through a discount or full-service broker. The discounter, however, may have a minimum purchase amount of a few thousand dollars and the full-service broker might have a minimum commission level, perhaps about $50 (if you buy him lunch or give his kid a ride home from soccer practice, he may waive his minimum and charge you less).

No matter how you make your initial purchase, once you are an official shareholder many companies offer a dividend reinvestment program (DRIP). This option is available from most companies that pay a cash dividend. Rather than have the company send your so-tiny-they-barely-cover-the-cost-of-the-stamp dividend checks to you or your brokerage account, you elect to have the company automatically purchase more shares for you or your child. Usually there is little or no cost to obtain shares in this manner.

Who Should Own the Shares?

The issue of ownership is especially important here because the stocks that *for sure* won't make your kid rich are the ones that are sold too soon. You should only purchase the stocks in the name of the child if you believe the following will be true:

- Her need of money for college will not force her to liquidate the portfolio
- She'll have the maturity to not sell the stocks as soon as she gains control of the account

If you are starting with a smaller amount of money that won't cause a tax liability (a few thousand dollars or less) you should own the stocks in your own name. If you are starting with a larger amount, or are fortunate enough to have the portfolio grow into the six-figure range, you might want to form a trust to hold the shares until the child is old enough to manage the money appropriately (see Chapter 12).

Successful common stock ownership is driven by "Ten Things You Need to Know," #1 (see page 38) and #10 (see page 46). You need to "fall in love" with these companies, because the longer your child can avoid selling them, the more likely they are to make her wealthy. And although the likelihood of picking a "rocket ship" is small, you can improve your child's chances by buying as many different companies as you can afford using the criteria above.

When times get tough or you need a little hope to hang on to your stocks, you can dream of the people who put $5,000 into Cisco Systems in the company's initial public offering in 1990 (and never sold). Ten years later their $5,000 had grown to over $5 million.

Advantages of Common Stock Investing

1. Low Initial Investment Most DSPs allow you to get started with as little as $100. This means you can develop a portfolio of ten stocks for as little as $1,000 (plus any fees), and can add to the positions (either directly or through DRIPs) with similar amounts.

2. Low Taxation The IRS requires you to pay taxes on capital gains, but only when you sell. The longer you hold these stocks, the longer you avoid paying any capital gains taxes, and can let your money accumulate. Unlike having your child's money invested in a mutual fund, *you* decide if and when to sell your holdings. And since you should only purchase common stocks if you and your child have a longer time horizon, if you do have to sell you will only pay the lower, long-term capital gains tax rate.

In addition, when selling shares your child has the right to designate *which* shares are being sold, for tax purposes. This means if she is in a higher tax bracket, she can designate the more recent (and likely higher-cost) purchases as the shares being sold. If she is in a lower tax bracket, she can designate shares with a lower cost basis as the ones sold.

3. Low Cost You can purchase stock through DSPs for as little as $5 per transaction. A full-service adviser may charge you at least $50 per trade, and a discount broker may not be much less. If you purchase shares via DRIPs, there is usually little or no charge.

4. Educational Opportunity Owning common stocks can have a two-pronged benefit for your child. Not only can you provide for her financial independence but you may spark an interest in a future career by using individual shares.

If you use a mutual fund or variable annuity, you and your child can still reap the benefits of common stock investing, but it will be harder for her to get excited about her money than if she were a "part owner" of a business.

Direct ownership of common shares gives your child a window into the world of business and finance. She can pick shares of companies she is familiar with, like McDonald's, the Gap, or Coca-Cola. She might learn more about an industry with which she is currently unacquainted. She can read the annual reports, and check the company's Web site for investor information. She can watch what news causes a stock price to go up or down, and how the overall movement of the stock market affects the price of her companies.

Disadvantages of Common Stock Investing

1. Poor Planning Tool Although direct ownership of common stocks can be a great way to enrich your child, it's not the best choice for goal-based planning. There is usually considerably more price fluctuation in the prices of one or two stocks than there is in a broadly diversified portfolio (like a mutual fund). That means that if you own shares in just a couple companies, you may vastly outperform "the market" over a long time, but your holdings may fall behind other investment alternatives for several years, too.

This can be detrimental to achieving any goals for your child that need to be reached within a specific time frame. Let's say it's the end of 1974, and you want to buy some stock for a newborn baby to pay for her college education. You have the foresight to know that with dividends reinvested, IBM will have an average annual return of about 8% over the next twenty-six years, so you put in $10,000.

How much do you have when your kid turns eighteen, at

the end of 1992? About $11,300, for an average annual return of less than 1%. In the meantime the cost of living has risen by an average of almost 6%, and the Standard & Poor's 500 index has averaged about 11%, according to Towers Data. You would have fared much better with a broadly diversified index fund.

That doesn't mean you can't use common stocks as an investment strategy to make a kid a millionaire (and indeed, from 1992 to the end of 2000 IBM gave its shareholders a ten-to-one return on their shares, for an average annual gain of over 36%!). But for targeted purposes, you may be better served by putting only a portion in common stocks and a larger amount in a growth mutual fund (see Chapter 1).

2. Possible Bookkeeping Nightmare If you are smart and disciplined, you will not only buy common stocks for your child, you will also accumulate shares systematically, when available. This means you will send in a dollar amount monthly, quarterly, or yearly to buy more shares (many DSPs offer this feature).

But when you go to sell these shares (or if the company is purchased in a cash buyout), you will owe taxes on the difference between what you sold the shares for, and what you paid for them. The IRS lets you choose from a few different ways to decide which shares were sold:

- First in, first out (FIFO)
- Average dollar cost
- Designated shares

Once you pick a particular method for cost-basis accounting, you've got to stick with that approach. You and your child have to keep the annual statement from any stock purchase plan, and remember which purchases you have designated as "sold." This is also true with any mutual fund you might choose, but in my experience the mutual funds have better systems in place to help you calculate your cost basis than direct stock purchase plans (see Chapter 1 for more information on cost basis, and designating shares when you sell).

3. Timing of the Trade When you purchase stock via a full-service or a discount broker, your trade is executed within seconds of your request. But purchasing via a DSP doesn't usually allow that type of immediacy. It can take weeks to process the order, and you won't know what price per share you paid until after the fact. Now, if you are a long-term, systematic investor, you probably don't care what price you pay (within a few bucks), but you need to be aware of this before you choose this investment method.

Some of the newer Web-based DSPs purchase stock several times per day. It doesn't guarantee you are going to make any more money, but at least you can have a better idea what price you are paying *before* you make your purchase.

4. Commission Costs Judged on a pure dollar basis, the $5 or so commission charged by DSPs doesn't seem like much to pay for a stock purchase. But if you only purchase $100 worth of stock and pay a $5 fee each time, you are paying 5% of your investment in handling fees, and you're not even getting any assistance for your extra dollars.

Try to save your deposits so you can contribute a larger dollar amount at each purchase. If you do, you'll lower the commission costs as a percentage of the purchase price.

5. Using DRIPs with Growth Companies In the last few years many growth-oriented companies have chosen to keep a greater share of their free cash for internal investment, rather than pay the money to shareholders in the form of dividends. Legendary growth companies of the 1990s like Microsoft and Cisco don't pay *any* dividends. This may be good for shareholders in the long run, but it means there is less money available to purchase shares through dividend reinvestment plans.

If there's going to be any new money to buy shares, it's going to come out of your pocket.

6. You're on Your Own One of the great things about common stock investing is that you don't have to pay any commission after the original purchase. You can accumulate hundreds of thousands of dollars of value over decades of ownership, and your total brokerage fees could be as low as $50 to $100. But you also can't expect constant handholding and attention from a financial adviser if you are only going to pay her a small amount of money over many years.

But that's okay. You and your child are going to be owning these stocks long after the broker has retired or changed careers, so it is up to you to keep on top of things.

College Factor

Although there is a potential for decent rates of tax-advantaged return by owning common stocks for the long term, you should think twice about buying shares to eventually pay for your child's college expenses. The volatility in prices in a diversified mutual fund can be hard enough to stomach; it would be tragic if your shares took a 50% dive a year or two before your kid enters college.

If you still decide to use common stocks to pay for college costs, you should sell the shares at least three years before your child graduates from high school, and put the proceeds in a money market account or certificate of deposit. Not only will you keep these gains from showing up as adjusted gross income for you or your child (reducing any financial aid you might receive), but you won't have to worry about the shares plummeting right before your child goes off to college.

Finally, keep the shares in your name, as it will lessen the amount of your Expected Family Contribution when your child's school calculates his financial aid package. If you have stocks with a lot of unrealized gains and you're thinking about using the proceeds for college, you can give the shares to your child and have her sell them. Her long-term capital gains tax rate will probably be lower than yours.

Getting Started

Securing your child's financial future through ownership of common stocks is a paradox in that it is both very difficult, and very easy. It's hard to know which stock to pick, and it can be demanding—especially if you have other plans for the money or worry about every short-term price swing.

But the easy part is that once you choose a publicly traded company, you can become a part owner for a few hundred dollars and a few minutes of your time. And if you can force yourself to "forget" you own the shares, you and your child may be rewarded with unfathomable long-term rates of growth, all while you barely lift a finger.

You can start right by following these steps:

1. Open Your Eyes Look around your community. Are there any widely admired publicly traded companies in your area? Do you have friends or family who work for a thriving organization? Ask them if they think you should purchase shares in the company. As you spend your money, stop and think if you would like to be on the *other* side of the counter, as a shareholder.

2. Do Your Homework Your local library will have tons of information on publicly traded companies. And for every item you find there, you will get a thousand bits of information from the Internet.

3. Make Your Purchase But don't suffer from "paralysis of overanalysis." Take a few hundred dollars (or whatever amount you won't miss—using a dollar amount that is relatively insignificant to you will keep you from worrying yourself into selling the stock), and buy shares in a company that you want to own. Buy two or three companies if you can afford it. If you make your purchase through a full-service or discount broker, you can expect to pay a minimum charge of anywhere from $40 to $100 for each purchase you make.

There are also some Web sites that have established relationships with thousands of publicly traded companies. The cost to enroll is minimal (if any), and through these sites you can research the companies and set up DSP plans with as many as you wish. You can check these sites out at:

> www.netstockdirect.com
> www.buyandhold.com
> www.sharebuilder.com
> www.moneypaper.com

4. *Don't* **Sell Your Stock!** You'll be tempted to get out when things get real good, and you will wish you *had* sold when things go south. Forget about it. People have made more money by owning shares in big, solid, boring companies (and never selling them) than have all the lottery winners, day traders, and dot-com entrepreneurs combined. The lazier you are, and the less attention you pay to the matter, the more likely that one or two of your blue-chip companies will emerge from the pack and become beloved members of your family.

PART THREE
Ages Thirteen Through Twenty-one

You now have a "mini adult" in your house, for better and for worse. You are getting a glimpse as to the type of person your child might become, and this can shape what type of investments are the most appropriate for you to make for your kid.

You also have college expenses staring you right in the face. Hopefully, you saved enough to at least get your child started. And while he is in school, checks for tuition expenses will probably be the only investment opportunities you have until he graduates.

If you are within three years of your child's going to college, be careful on two fronts. First, make sure that you sell any appreciated assets well before you fill out financial aid forms, so the sales proceeds don't jack up your adjusted gross income. Second, move the college money portfolio into a greater cash position. If the market gets crunched and you're fully invested, it could quickly knock out 30% of your accumulation just when you need it.

If you do have some extra money and a low tolerance for fluctuation, the zero coupon bonds discussed in Chapter 7 should give you a calmer journey to your child's financial independence. And since your earnings are probably higher than they have ever been in your life, you've been bumped up into a higher tax bracket. If you plan on keeping the money in your own name for a while, tax-free zero coupon bonds can give you solid and predictable after-tax returns.

Once your child begins earning any money whatsoever, you are ready to take a look at a Roth IRA for him, discussed in Chapter 8. You should certainly encourage him to put his own money in this type of account. But if you can't convince him to start worrying about his retirement, you can still put your own money in his Roth IRA (this is one place for your dollars that is so powerful, it might justify diverting a few thousand dollars from paying for college so that you have enough for a decent-sized deposit, and making up the difference with a student loan).

chapter seven

The Worry Wart's Way to Make a Kid a Millionaire

Slow and Steady, Using Zero Coupon Bonds

I f the idea of a roller-coaster ride on the stock market makes you jittery, the merry-go-round method might be a little more your style. If you need security, safety, and predictability to sleep at night, look to bonds. Zero coupon bonds.

"Zero coupon" refers to the way interest is paid on a type of debt instrument. Usually when an investor purchases a bond he gets a series of set interest payments over a period of time, until he receives the bond face value at maturity and the interest payment stream stops.

Zero coupon bonds (also called "accrual" bonds) pay no interest payments. Instead, the investor buys the bonds for a fraction of face value—say, 50 cents on the dollar—and when the bond matures the investor receives the face value of the bond. It's kind of like a balloon payment on a mortgage.

Zero coupon bonds allow you to put a small amount of money in now, with the expectation of receiving a larger amount at some time in the future. For example, for about $1,741, you can purchase a bond with a $10,000 face value (meaning you will get $10,000 when the bond comes due), earning 6%, and maturing in thirty years.

This feature makes zero coupon bonds a neat planning tool.

If you have a particular goal in mind and know roughly when you will need the money (say, your kid's freshman year in college), you can purchase a bond maturing when your child turns eighteen.

This type of investment also lends itself well to a bond purchase technique known as "laddering." Laddering refers to buying bonds that mature in a period of successive years. For example, let's say you want a newborn child to have $20,000 coming due each year for four years, starting when he turns eighteen. If the bonds each pay 6%, your ladder would look something like this:

Child's Age	Maturity Amount	Your Cost Today
18	$20,000	$ 7,007
19	20,000	6,611
20	20,000	6,237
21	20,000	5,884
Totals:	**$80,000**	**$25,739**

If your child doesn't need to spend the maturing proceeds of a bond, laddering can help him manage interest rate fluctuation. Let's say the first bond comes due on his eighteenth birthday. If he doesn't need the money, he can *reinvest* the $20,000 in a bond coming due on his twenty-second birthday. If the current interest rates (also known as "bond yields") have fallen by the time the first bond matures, he will still have three more bonds earning a higher interest rate. If bond yields have risen, he will have money coming due that will allow him to take advantage of the increase in interest rates.

When it comes to investing for a child, the three most attractive zero coupon bond investment methods are savings bonds, zero coupon Treasuries, and tax-free municipal bonds.

Savings Bonds

In post–World War II America the most popular method for saving on behalf of a child were savings bonds issued by the United States government. A generation of investors were already used to buying bonds to support the war effort, and still had the 1929 stock market crash fresh on their minds. These bonds were viewed as consumer friendly, conservative ways to save.

Not much about the bonds has changed in the last sixty years. What has changed is the decreased popularity of the bonds relative to other types of investments, especially stocks and mutual funds. Although the long-term growth prospects of common stock mutual funds usually make them better investments for a child than bonds, that doesn't mean you should ignore savings bonds completely.

The type of savings bond that is usually most suitable for children is the Series EE bonds, which are available at thousands of banks and financial institutions around the country. They are backed by the full faith and credit of the United States government, making them one of the safest investments around. You can buy them with as little as $25 for a $50 face value bond, and you can purchase as much as $15,000 ($30,000 face value) of Series EE savings bonds in a given year.

The interest rate on Series EE bonds is set on May 1 and November 1 of each year. The rate is 90% of the average interest rate of the five-year Treasury note over the previous six months. Since the rate is reset every six months, you won't be able to know right off the bat when you will get your $50 (the higher the rates go, the sooner your bond will mature), only that you *will* get it within seventeen years. Even after it hits the $50 mark, the bonds can continue to pay interest for thirty years, after which you have to redeem them or convert them to Series HH bonds.

The interest from Series EE bonds is exempt from state and

local income taxes. In addition, savings bonds may also be exempt from federal income taxes if the proceeds are used for tuition expenses for a postsecondary institution, subject to certain restrictions (see page 172). For tax purposes you can choose between declaring the interest earned annually, or when the bonds mature (or are cashed in).

You can redeem Series EE bonds as early as six months after purchase; however, there is a penalty of three months' interest for any bonds redeemed fewer than five years after purchase.

Advantages of Savings Bonds

1. Safety The full faith and credit of the United States government is as good a guarantee as your child is going to get.

2. Low Minimum Investment There are very few investment opportunities that you can purchase for as little as $25, and that are available at the lobbies and drive-up lanes of just about every financial institution in the country ("When you get done with your ballet lesson, we can stop for some *savings bonds* on the way home!").

3. Adjusting Yield The interest rate resets every six months. Consequently, if you purchase a savings bond at a time when interest rates are low, you don't have to worry about "locking in" that low rate if interest rates eventually go back up.

4. Flexible Tax Options You can choose to pay the taxes either annually as the bond grows in value, or upon maturity. This means that if you can correctly guess your child's tax status over the life of the bond, you can then choose which method would be the most advantageous to use.

If you are buying a savings bond for a young child, but don't expect it to be used for tuition, it is generally better to declare the interest annually from the start. Here's why: for a child under fourteen, the first $750 of interest is tax-free and the next $750 is taxed at his rate (in 2001). By the time the bond matures, your child may be working and may be at a higher income tax rate.

---

5. College Tuition Payments Under certain circumstances, interest from a Series EE savings bond is exempt not only from state and local taxes, but also from federal taxes, if the following conditions are met:

- The bond was purchased after January 1, 1990
- The purchaser must be at least twenty-four years old before the bond's issue date
- The funds are used for tuition only; not room, board, or books
- Income limits in the year the bond is redeemed—in 2001 the single taxpayer had to have less than $55,570 in modified adjusted gross income, or $83,650 for couples. The tax advantage is gradually reduced beginning at these levels, and disappears completely at $70,750 for singles and $113,650 for married taxpayers filing jointly

Disadvantages of Savings Bonds

1. Low Rate of Return These are real snoozers when it comes to making money over the long haul. If you have a long time frame for your child, you may be better served by investing in common stocks, either directly or through mutual funds.

2. Unpredictability Just because your money is safe, it doesn't mean *all* the thrill has been removed from the investment. Because of the fluctuating interest rate you still don't know when you will get the face value of a Series EE bond, other than within the seventeen-year guarantee. This may make it difficult for you to have a certain amount of money assured on a certain date.

3. Complexity Savings bonds are supposed to be simple, easy ways for anyone to grow money, but you have to remember that these bonds are administered by the U.S. Treasury, the same people who designed the income tax system for your convenience and pleasure. You can get help at just about any financial institution that sells the bonds, but the myriad of options and limits available to current and past bond purchasers has caused many well-meaning investors to throw up their hands in disgust.

4. Tuition Restrictions Not only is the federal exemption from taxation restricted to just tuition payments, but only those at four-year and certain two-year institutions. So if your child wants to become a radio DJ, for example, you would still have to pay federal tax on the interest of the bond, even if he uses it to pay his broadcasting school bills.

The income restrictions are even more frustrating. Although adjusted annually for inflation, the limits on income are set for the year the bonds are cashed, not for the year they are purchased. That means you could start buying bonds for your newborn child and accumulate thousands of dollars in face value bonds by the time he is eighteen. Heaven forbid, though, that you and your spouse are earning a decent amount of money when your child tries to use the bonds to pay for tuition. Because if your income exceeds the limits established in the year the bonds are redeemed, about one third of the appreciation of those bonds will go toward federal income taxes.

Getting Started

You can call 1-800-4US-BOND, go to www.savingsbond. gov on the Web, or visit your local financial institution.

Zero Coupon Treasuries

If you have a little more money to invest or you want a guaranteed amount of money exactly on a certain date, zero coupon Treasury bonds may be better suited for your child than savings bonds.

Back in the late 1970s some enterprising financial minds realized they could buy a normal interest-bearing Treasury bond at face value, rip the coupons off, and sell the bond at a steep discount from its face value. They then would be able to legally to take the "loss" on the face value, save themselves a corresponding amount in taxes, yet still collect the interest payment from the coupons. The Treasury Department closed the tax loophole in 1982, but by then investors were enamored with the couponless bonds. Today billions of dollars' worth of zero coupon Treasuries are bought and sold every day.

Like Series EE savings bonds, zero coupon Treasury bonds are backed by the full faith and credit of the United States government, making them one of the safest investments available to you and your child. Interest earned by Treasury bonds is also exempt from state and local taxes.

But that is where the similarities end. Zero coupon Treasuries are not sold directly by the government. They must be purchased through a broker, either discount or full-service. The minimum purchase is $1,000 face value, but some brokers may require a slightly higher minimum. The interest rate you receive is locked in from the moment you purchase the bond. You can also pick which year and month you want the bonds to come due. When you purchase the bond you will receive an "accretion schedule," which will show you the year-by-year automatic dollar growth in the value of the bond. This yearly appreciation schedule is what you use to determine your annual federal tax liability.

The initial price you pay depends on what prevailing interest rates are at the time you make the purchase. And the fluctuation in interest rates can be both to your advantage and your disadvantage.

Let's say you have a newborn child, and you want to have $10,000 coming due for him in thirty years. You check to see what government bonds are paying, and find out the current annual interest rate for thirty-year Treasuries is 6.5%. You agree to buy ten $1,000 bonds, and your initial transaction looks something like this:

$$\text{Ten bonds} \times \$152 \text{ per bond} = \$1,520$$

Two years later, you decide to buy ten more $1,000 (face value) bonds for your child, again maturing when he turns thirty. Your broker tells you that the current interest rate for twenty-eight-year Treasuries is now 8%, and you agree to buy ten more $1,000 bonds. This time your transaction looks like this:

$$\text{Ten bonds} \times \$116 \text{ per bond} = \$1,160$$

Why did you pay $360 less this time, even though you have two years less time for the bonds to appreciate? The answer is the change in current interest rates. The value of existing bonds moves in the opposite direction from interest rates. When interest rates are rising, the value of your bond portfolio goes down. When interest rates are falling, the value of your bond portfolio goes up.

Sometimes this concept can be a little confusing, so it might help you if I return once again to the seesaw to illustrate:

Interest rates   Bond prices

Whether interest rates move up or down after you purchase the bond, you are always assured of getting your $1,000 back on the maturity date. But if you need to sell the bonds before the maturity date, you may get more or less than the accreted value (see "accretion schedule," page 173), depending on how long you have held the bond and what interest rates have done since you purchased it.

If you sell the bond for a price above the accreted value, you have to pay capital gains taxes on the amount above the accreted value. If the price is below the accreted value, you can declare a loss on the difference between the accreted value and your price.

Unlike savings bonds, you have no choice as to when you or your child pays taxes on the accrued interest of a zero coupon Treasury. You have to pay federal taxes each year on the interest earned according to the accretion schedule, even though there is no actual cash flowing to you or your child.

Advantages of Zero Coupon Treasuries

1. Safety The backing of the United States government makes these the most reliable investments you can buy.

2. Yield Treasuries usually pay higher pretax yields than savings bonds or tax-free bonds of similar quality.

3. Predictability Because a zero coupon Treasury bond always has a specific maturity date, you will know exactly how much money will come due at an exact time. This allows you to purchase these bonds for a specific purpose like paying for college or a home purchase, and you can rest assured that the money will be there.

Perhaps you know you should be in common stocks to get the best long-term return for your child, but you are unsettled by the ups and downs of the stock market. Combining these predictable bonds with stocks or stock mutual funds can alleviate your anxiety.

Say you have $10,000 to invest for a child, and your child will need the money in eighteen years. Buy a zero coupon bond with the face value of your original overall investment

($10,000). Take the rest of the money and put it in a growth mutual fund. If the yield on an eighteen-year Treasury bond is 6%, your initial transaction would look like this:

Ten $1,000 bonds at $350	$ 3,500
Growth mutual fund	6,500
Total	$10,000

This means that even if the entire value of the growth mutual fund disappears (it won't), you will at least get your initial $10,000 deposit back in eighteen years. Chances are, though, that the growth mutual fund will not only remain intact, it will even outperform the Treasury bond. Then you will have a higher overall annual return than 6%, yet not be as scared by swings in the value of the growth fund.

4. Perpetual Ladder Treasuries are always available for purchase, giving you some flexibility of action when the bonds mature. Let's say you are trying to build wealth for a newborn baby. Today, you purchase a bond with a certain maturity length (say, twenty-five years). If the interest rate is 6%, you can purchase $20,000 (face value) of bonds for about $4,660. Next year, you could do the same thing, and so on until you have accumulated $20,000 coming due every year from the time your child turns twenty-five until he turns thirty-five.

Each year when the bonds come due, your child can evaluate if he needs to spend the proceeds for something. But if he doesn't have a use for the money, he can use the money to purchase new bonds. If he chooses to buy thirty-year zero coupon Treasuries (again paying 6%), his new laddered portfolio will give him almost $115,000 coming due *each year* from the ages of fifty-five to sixty-four, for a total matured amount of $1,149,000!

Disadvantages of Zero Coupon Treasuries

1. Low Rate of Return Because Treasuries are extremely safe and conservative, the interest rate is lower than the historical rate of return for common stocks. In fact, in periods of high in-flation, you might find yourself losing purchasing power on the money in the bond, if the inflation rate is higher than the in-terest rate of the bond.

In addition, if you are investing for a particular goal for a child, bonds may not grow as fast as the price of your goal. For instance, some experts predict that the cost of a college educa-tion will rise at a rate of 7% per year or more, meaning if you own a bond paying less than the inflation rate, you are losing ground every year.

2. Taxation Treasuries are exempt from all state and local taxes, but not federal. This is not an issue if the interest is taxed at the 15% bracket, or if the bonds are held in an IRA. But if the inter-est is going to be taxed at the 27% bracket or higher, you may be better off going with tax-free zero coupon bonds (see page 178). Tax-free bonds usually pay a lower pretax yield than similar Treasuries, but since the holder pays no taxes on the interest, the after-tax yield may be much higher. In addition, because zero coupon Treasuries pay no interest annually, you've got to come up with extra money out-of-pocket to pay each year's tax bill.

3. Price Fluctuations Although you are guaranteed a Treasury bond's face value at maturity, you have no such assurance if you need to sell the bond before it comes due. What you will get is the market value of the bond, for better or worse. This means you have to call up a discount or full-service broker and find out what other investors are willing to pay for a bond like yours. If you've owned the bond for a long time or interest rates have declined since your original purchase, you should be in the black.

If interest rates have risen, however, you may get substan-tially less than you put in, especially if the bond's maturity is still a long way away (see the "seesaw" example above).

Getting Started

Since zero coupon Treasuries are not available to be purchased directly from the government, you have to call either a discount or full-service broker. You can find current yield quotes through most financial Web sites and newspapers. You can also read a helpful description of STRIPS (the government's acronym for zero coupon Treasury bonds) at www. publicdebt.treas.gov/of/ofstrips.htm.

Tax-Free Zero Coupon Bonds

Under the federal income tax law, entities such as states, cities, counties, and school districts can raise money by issuing bonds. The bonds usually pay a lower interest rate than Treasuries, but are also exempt from federal (and in some cases state) taxation.

Like Treasuries, tax-free municipal bonds have been available in zero coupon form for years. You purchase these bonds from either a discount broker or a full-service adviser. You buy the bond at a deep discount from its face value, and at maturity you receive one lump sum equal to your principal, plus interest compounded semiannually at the original interest rate. The bonds are usually available with a minimum purchase of $5,000 face value (although some firms are beginning to require $10,000 minimum face value for purchase). Subsequent bonds can be bought in $5,000 face value increments.

Tax-free zero coupon bonds are basically a loan to the issuing organization. You are giving the city, state, or school district money for either general use or a specific project, and are relying on the ability of the issuer to pay you back at the agreed-upon interest rate, and upon maturity. Some bonds are callable, meaning the issuer has the right to pay you your principal and interest before the maturity date. Pay close attention to any call features in a bond, as they can affect the price and marketability of the security.

How do you know if the issuing organization will be able to pay you back? Well, most large bond issuers pay two services—Moody's and Standard & Poor's—to issue ratings for a particular bond issue. The ratings are as follows:

Safety	Moody's	Standard & Poor's
Prime	Aaa	AAA
Excellent	Aa	AA
Upper medium	A	A
Lower medium	Baa	BBB
Speculative	Ba	BB
Very speculative	B,Caa	B,CCC,CC
Default	Ca,C	D

Generally, the higher the rating an issuer has, the lower the interest rate and the yield is likely to be.

Moody's and Standard & Poor's also keep an eye on the issuer after the initial sale, and may upgrade or downgrade their rating based on changes in the issuer's financial situation. Some issuers purchase private insurance that guarantees bondholders will get their investment principal plus interest. These insured tax-free bonds almost always receive "AAA" ratings.

Some bond issues are nonrated, usually because the issue is too small to justify hiring a rating agency. This doesn't mean the issuing organization is necessarily unsafe, just that you will have to do your own homework on the credit quality of the issuer. The best way to do this is by reading the prospectus, a document providing the legal and financial details behind the issue.

The yield of tax-free zero coupon bonds is usually a tad lower than the interest on Treasuries or other comparable debt securities. Yet many investors still prefer tax-free bonds because their after-tax yield can be substantially higher.

How do you decide? A simple equation can tell you:

$$\frac{\text{Tax-free interest rate}}{1 - (\text{Federal tax rate})} = \text{Taxable equivalent yield}$$

Let's say you are buying a bond for a child in the 15% tax bracket. The bond yields 5%. Your taxable equivalent yield would be as follows:

$$\frac{.05}{1 - .15} = .0588, \text{ or } 5.88\%$$

You can probably do better than 5.88% by buying a taxable bond, such as a Treasury. But let's say the bond is being purchased for someone in the 27% bracket. Then the taxable equivalent yield would be calculated like this:

$$\frac{.05}{1 - .27} = .0685, \text{ or } 6.85\%$$

That might be competitive with similar taxable bonds. And obviously, the higher the tax bracket, the more attractive tax-free bonds become. For instance, an investor in a 36% bracket earning 5% tax-free would need a taxable bond paying 7.8% to equal his after-tax yield.

This difference is even more dramatic if you are able to find a bond that is exempt from both federal and state taxes. Usually bonds issued in your home state might also be exempt from your state's income tax (it's best to check each bond to be sure). If you are in a 36% tax bracket and have a 7% state income tax, your 5% bond exempt from state and federal taxes gives you a taxable equivalent yield of 8.8%. This rate of return rivals the hypothetical 10% long-term return many people expect from common stocks.

As with Treasuries, purchasers of tax-free zero coupon bonds receive an accretion schedule at the time of the initial purchase. This accretion schedule is generated so investors can declare any interest that is taxable at the state level, if applicable. Accreted interest must be declared each year, whether or not it is taxable.

Zero coupon tax-free bonds can be sold at any time, but like Treasuries, sellers receive the market price for the bonds, for better or worse. This means you may sell the bond for an amount above or below the accreted value, depending on a few factors:

- Whether interest rates have moved up or down since you purchased the bond
- How long you have owned the bond
- Whether income tax rates have gone up or down since you purchased the bond
- Any changes in the rating of the bond issuer

If you sell the bond for a price above the accreted value, you'll owe capital gains taxes on the amount above the accreted value. If the price is below the accreted value, you can declare a loss on the difference between the accreted value and your price.

Advantages of Tax-Free Zero Coupon Bonds

1. Control Usually you are confronted with a choice when you are deciding to invest money for the benefit of a child. You can either keep the money in your name, maintaining control and also having the gains and income taxed at your (usually) higher rate. Or, you can put the money in the child's name and have gains and income taxed at the lower rate of the child. But if you choose to do that, legally the money is your kid's, and once he reaches the age of majority he can do whatever he pleases with the money, regardless of your wishes (see Chapter 12). Plus, when your child's college figures his yearly financial aid package, 35% of a $10,000 bond in his name will be counted toward your Expected Family Contribution, versus only about $600 of the same amount held in your name.

Tax-free zero coupon bonds offer you a way to keep the assets in your name, yet not worry about increasing your tax bill. Plus, you can use the flexibility of the laddered portfolio to meet the needs of your child.

Let's say you have a newborn baby for whom you wish to provide financial security. You want to help him afford major lifetime expenses, but because you have no idea as to how soon (if ever) he will be mature enough to handle money as you deem appropriate, you are also leery of giving the money to him directly. You can buy tax-free zero coupon bonds in your own name, with maturities scheduled to coincide with prominent events in his life (entering college, turning twenty-one, buying a house, etc.).

If he were born in the year 2002, and you wished to have $20,000 coming due at the ages of eighteen, twenty-one, and twenty-five, for example, your laddered bond portfolio would look something like this (assuming a 5% yield on all the bonds):

Maturity Year	Initial Purchase	Maturing Proceeds
2020	$ 8,311	$20,000
2023	7,179	20,000
2027	5,906	20,000
Totals	$21,396	$60,000

Fast-forward to the year 2020. The boy is graduating from high school with honors, sings in the choir, and is on the track team. He hardly gives you any trouble, and by all accounts is a good, solid kid. He is entering college, and could use a little help. You happily give him a check for $20,000 and tell him if he stays in school you may be able to help him out again in a few years.

But what if things aren't quite so rosy? What if he wants to bike across China, and you don't feel like subsidizing his trip (although many parents or grandparents would)? Go ahead and roll the maturing bond into another tax-free zero coupon bond, maybe one maturing when he turns thirty. Every time another bond comes due, you'll have the opportunity to sit down with him, discuss where he is at in his life, and decide if he is ready to handle the check you are considering giving to him. Hopefully, he's maturing at least as fast as the bonds are! If not, keep rolling the bonds into future years until he is ready to manage the money properly.

And what if he never reaches that point? What if this angelic little boy grows up to be a drug-pushing Hell's Angel with a snake tattoo on his face? Ignoring your disappointment (unless you *also* happen to belong to the Hell's Angels), you will be especially glad you chose to buy tax-free zero coupon bonds and keep them in your name. You have absolutely no obligation, legally or morally, to give him the money. You can pick one of this miscreant's brothers or sisters, a different family member, or even a well-deserving charity. Best of all, *you* can even keep the money, and splurge on a midlife crisis car.

2. Tax-Free Status This feature doesn't mean much if you are helping a child in a low tax bracket, or are funding an account with a small amount of money. But if your financial largesse will earn money that will be taxed at the 27% (or higher) bracket, tax-free bonds may give you and your child a much higher after-tax return.

If you want to buy zero coupon bonds in the name of a child but you don't know which ones to buy, try this: If he is under the age of fourteen, buy Treasuries, as long as the annual interest generated will be less than $1,500 ($25,000 of Treasuries paying 6% yields $1,500 in annual interest). If he is older than fourteen and in the 15% tax bracket, definitely stick to Treasuries. If he's in a higher tax bracket, or you expect him to be soon, buy zero coupon tax-free bonds. And remember, you can always sell one type of bond to buy another if the child's tax status changes.

Disadvantages of Tax-Free Zero Coupon Bonds

1. Low Before-Tax Yield Tax-free zero coupon bonds usually have the lowest yield of all comparable investments.

2. Relatively Low Liquidity Although you can buy tax-free zero coupon bonds from thousands of brokers and dealers, you are usually limited to buying from a particular firm's inventory. This means if you are looking for a bond with a specific maturity or credit rating, you may have to either call around to different firms, or have a broker keep an eye out for a bond that meets your criteria.

This will also be a factor if you or your child needs to sell the bond before it matures. Theoretically, you can receive more or less than the accreted value of a tax-free zero coupon bond if you sell it before maturity, depending on the factors listed in the above description. But because it is harder to match buyers and sellers of tax-free bonds than other types of investments, you are at the mercy of the broker. Shop around to find the best bid before you decide.

Getting Started

This table may help you decide which zero coupon bonds are best for you, depending on your priorities:

Priority	Savings Bonds	Treasuries	Tax-Frees
• Low initial investment	X		
• Higher pretax return		X	

Priority	Savings Bonds	Treasuries	Tax-Frees
• Higher after-tax return			X
• Inflation protection	X		
• Easy liquidity	X	X	
• Targeted maturity dates		X	X
• College saving in your name	X		X
• College saving in child's name		X	

chapter eight

On the Paper Route to Prosperity

It Doesn't Matter Whose Money Goes into Your Kid's Roth IRA, Only That It Does!

Please turn to the dedication page at the beginning of this book. See those beautiful young women in the picture? That's my wife, Rachel, and my daughter, Ellie. Rachel agreed to work for free, but I paid Ellie $2,000 to model for this along with some other advertising items (I think I got a good deal).

For now Ellie is too young to have much say about where her money goes, but Rachel and I think that one day she will be happy we deposited the $2,000 in a Roth IRA in Ellie's name. If that account earns 10% annually and no other deposits or withdrawals are made, by the time Ellie is sixty-seven years old she will be able to withdraw over *$1,000,000*. And she will never, ever, pay a single penny in federal taxes on that money.

The significance of these numbers is overwhelming. Ellie would have to make $2,000 Roth IRA contributions for herself *each year* from the ages of 26 to 67 to end up with the same amount of money, assuming the account earns 10% annually. Our $2,000 contribution today has the same power as her $82,000 worth of contributions over that forty-one-year period.

Like most people, you may have never even considered opening a Roth IRA for your child. Sometimes this is because she is not eligible—after all, she must have legitimate earned income at least equal to the amount of the deposit into the Roth IRA. And unlike me, you may not have an opportunity to pay your toddler wages.

But it is very likely that your child will earn some form of income by the time she reaches her mid-teens. And whether that income is from baby-sitting, selling shoes at the mall, or working for you, you must not miss the opportunity to use this income to make your kid a millionaire.

I've never raised a teenager, but I was one a long time ago. And I recognize that it's almost impossible to get a kid thinking about the next five *days*, much less five decades. Chances are, you are not going to be able to convince your child to put her paychecks into a Roth IRA. She may even be saving her money for a new bike, a trip to Europe, or the latest video game.

No problem.

You can use your *own* money to make the contributions, as long as you don't put in more than she earns, and don't go past the annual contribution limit.

Why Not a Regular IRA?

Because of its tax-free withdrawals and flexibility, when we're talking about a teenager's income a Roth IRA clobbers a regular IRA every time.

Once your child is an adult, she will probably participate in a work-sponsored retirement plan by contributing pretax dollars. This will lower her taxable income at the time of deposit, but she will have to pay taxes on the earnings when she begins making withdrawals.

But as a teenager, her income will be so low and her taxes so insignificant, that there's virtually no benefit to depositing pretax dollars into a retirement account. So depositing $2,000 into a Roth IRA instead of a deductible IRA will not cost her much (if anything) in today's tax dollars. But if that $2,000 deposit grows to $250,000, having it in a Roth IRA versus a deductible IRA could save her over $70,000 in taxes at retirement, if she is in a 28% income tax bracket when she begins making with-drawals.

What Is "Legitimate" Income?

Before you can contribute to your child's Roth IRA, you need to know what types of income the IRS considers to be "legitimate." Depending on the age of the child in question, she can earn money working outside the home, for you if you are self-employed, or even by performing tasks in your own home.

When Your Child Works Outside Your Home

As your child enters her teenage years she will be tempted by the thought of picking up some extra money. According to recent Bureau of Labor statistics, over 40% of high school students are employed outside the home. Your child will see other kids spending their earnings, and she will probably want to join them in the ranks of the gainfully employed.

Like most parents, you probably won't discourage her from getting a job. First of all, your family may need the extra income! You also may be tired of forking over your money for movies, electronics, and "must-have" clothing items and would like her to share in the expense of her material pursuits. Finally, you may believe that working during her teen years will teach her to get along with others, accept responsibility, and build a work history that will help her eventually get a great full-time job.

Once your kid is ready to begin working, she can decide what kind of work she wants to do. Working for a formal employer (like a supermarket or restaurant) means she will get more structure and training; however, with those benefits also comes a more inflexible work schedule. But at least these types of employers will take care of all the necessary paperwork and withholding applicable to the situation. She will need to file a tax return if she wants to get a refund of any taxes her employer withheld.

But what if your child is an enterprising sort and wants to

go into business for herself? As strange as that may sound, it is actually more likely that your child's first earnings will come not from flipping burgers, but rather from mowing lawns, washing cars, delivering newspapers, or baby-sitting (some studies have said up to 90% of all teenage girls have received payment for baby-sitting—but try finding one for this Saturday night). The great thing about performing services for other people is that your child gets to decide when and for whom she will work, what her rate will be, and what types of jobs she enjoys doing most.

If your child chooses this route, you would think she is self-employed. But when she is performing a personal service or household chore for a neighbor, for tax purposes she is really working for the person who is paying her. That said, it is still a good idea for you and your child to document any cash payments she receives, if you are going to use the earnings as the basis for a Roth IRA contribution.

If your child has more than $400 of annual net income from odd jobs, and the people paying her don't withhold any Social Security or Medicare taxes, she must file a tax return and pay self-employment tax.

It's not that hard to get your kid a few dollars of legitimate income. America loves an entrepreneur, and if your kid goes around your neighborhood offering to baby-sit or mow lawns, my guess is that she'll have more than enough opportunities to become a mini mogul.

Working for a Self-Employed Parent

If you (or your spouse) have your own business, you have a very flexible way to pay your child and contribute to a Roth IRA on her behalf. The job doesn't have to be anything special—it can be cleaning an office, assembling a mailing campaign, or whatever else you might need done. The main requirement is that your child be paid a reasonable wage for her work.

What is the definition of the term "reasonable"? Well, there are no strict government guidelines, but if you would only pay the wage in question to your own flesh and blood, it's probably too high. (One former boss told me, "The only fair wage is one where both the employee and employer feel cheated.") However, when some fast-food outlets are paying $10 per hour to start (and still not filling the positions), it would be difficult to argue that a wage in that ballpark would be outlandish.

Child Labor Laws One word of caution about employing your child: As you are going to need to document the days and hours she has worked, be careful not to run afoul of the child labor laws. Businesses not engaged in interstate commerce or with revenues of less than $500,000 are exempt from these laws. But if your business does not fall under these exemptions, you should pay attention.

According to the Fair Labor Standards Act of 1938, your child must be at least sixteen to be employed in work that doesn't involve agriculture. Children ages fourteen and fifteen can work outside of school hours in a few general occupations, like retail and restaurant service. Children of any age can perform the following duties: deliver newspapers; perform in radio, TV, movies, or the theater; work for their parents in any solely owned nonfarm, nonhazardous business; or gather evergreens and make evergreen wreaths (I'm not sure where the last one comes from; probably the result of high-pressure, big-money lobbyists from the holiday decorations industry).

One of the best opportunities a self-employed person has to help a child earn income is how Rachel and I did it: Use pictures of your kid in advertising and promotion, where appropriate.

In addition to the types of work that children are allowed to perform, the number of hours they can work is also regulated.

The amount of hours permitted are raised as the child gets older:

Age	Restrictions
18 and over	Any job for unlimited hours
16 and 17	Any nonhazardous job for unlimited hours
14 and 15	No mining, manufacturing, or hazardous jobs, no more than 3 hours on a school day, no more than 18 hours in a school week, no more than 8 hours on a non-school day, or 40 hours in a nonschool week. Children in this age range also cannot begin working before 7 A.M. or work after 7 P.M. during the school year, and can't work past 9 P.M. from June 1 to Labor Day.

Your business might be exempt from many of these laws. And even if it isn't, I'm not saying that if you are a self-employed business owner and your kid vacuums your office once a week, jackbooted government agents are going to kick down the door and rifle through your records. But if you are self-employed, chances are you are going to be audited one day. If the IRS finds out you violated any of the child labor laws, the Department of Labor can hit you with a penalty of up to $10,000 per child employee.

Save Yourself Some Taxes If you are self-employed, unincorporated, and your child is under eighteen, you can not only use the Roth IRA to make her a millionaire, you can also save yourself thousands of dollars in taxes.

Here's how.

If your income is under the upper limit for deducting Social Security payments ($80,400 for the 2001 tax year), every dollar you pay your child reduces your own Social Security and Medicare taxes by 15.3% of the amount paid to the child. For instance, if you pay your child $3,000 per year to get the maximum Roth IRA contribution allowed in 2002 through 2004, and you would normally earn $65,000 from your business, your tax savings would look like this:

Social Security taxes	$ 372
Medicare taxes	87
Federal income taxes (27%)	810
State income taxes (7%)	210
Total savings each year	$1,479

In this situation, paying your child $3,000 to work for you will save you well over $1,000 in taxes. And for every $3,000 you put in your teenager's Roth IRA, she will have over $350,000 in fifty years (assuming a 10% annual return) that she can withdraw free from federal taxes!

Working Around the House

So your kid is too young to work at McDonald's, and you aren't self-employed. How else can you help her earn some income so that contributions can be made to her Roth IRA? Common sense would tell you that if you are paying her to clean the house, mow the lawn, or shovel your sidewalks, then that's income to her. If it's income to her, you can use that as the basis for a Roth IRA contribution, right?

Paying your child yourself, and then using that income as the basis for a contribution to her Roth IRA is a "gray" area in the tax code. Proponents of this practice argue that if your kid can use payments from your neighbor to fund a Roth IRA she sure can use payments from *you* to do the same thing.

But those who say the law doesn't allow us to base Roth IRA contributions on allowance and household chore money point out that although the IRS taxes a lot of things, it doesn't tax allowance money paid from a parent to a child. Since it isn't taxed, the income can't be used as the basis for a Roth IRA con-tribution.

The IRS has been mute on the subject so far. And it may never challenge the idea of your giving your kid $20 a week to make her bed and mow the lawn, then making equal contributions to a Roth IRA. But if you do choose to use what looks like allowance money, and payments for performance of regular household duties as the basis to contribute to a Roth IRA, and the IRS subsequently rules against your justification, you or your child could be in for a financial mess.

If the IRS discovers an improper payment was made to a Roth IRA, the penalty can be as much as 6% of the deposit amount, charged for each year the money remained in the account. Plus, your child could be forced to liquidate the account, and would owe back taxes and penalties on all of the earnings that had accumulated. Not exactly the kind of incident that looks good on a college application.

How can you make sure you stay on the right side of the law? Well, first of all, forget about using the allowance money you give your child as the basis for a contribution. Second, don't let this ambiguity discourage you from using income your child receives from someone other than you—there is no question as to the legality of that practice. Finally, you should still be able to make Roth IRA contributions for your child on the basis of money paid for larger projects, such as painting or helping to refinish the basement. If there's nothing to do around your own house, talk to your kid's grandparents about having her perform chores and tasks for them.

No matter how old your child is, one "end around" way to get a Roth IRA for her is to have her grandparents open an account for *themselves,* and make her the beneficiary. But they're retired? No sweat—pay them babysitting money when they take care of your kid, and then use the money as the basis to open their Roth IRA. When they pass away, your child will have to begin withdrawing from the inherited Roth IRA. But the minimum withdrawal amount will be so small that the account should still grow into a big source of tax-free income for her (see Chapter 13).

Regardless of what duties you are paying your child to perform, you should keep the following recommendations in mind when you are employing your child for duties in your home:

- Pay her a reasonable wage for her work.
- Keep complete, accurate, and detailed records of the dates, wages, hours worked, and duties performed.
- Write checks to your child for the wages performed. This will establish a "paper trail" to document your child's earnings.

And of course, you need to make sure you address any self-employment tax (page 189) or income tax obligations (page 293) your working child might have.

Establishing a Roth IRA for Your Child

Once your child has a job and earned income, you are free to establish a Roth IRA for her. Keep these points in mind as you go about it:

1. Timing You don't have to establish the Roth IRA until April 15 of the year following the one in which your child has earnings. This is a good time, though, to invoke "Ten Things You Need to Know," #1 (see page 38). Few people are aware that you can make contributions to a Roth IRA even before you earn the money, and making them sooner rather than later can mean tens of thousands of dollars more for your child at retirement.

For example, let's say it's January 2, 2002. You expect your kid to begin earning income this year, and that it will be at least $2,000. You are free to immediately make a $2,000 contribution for the 2002 tax year, even though she hasn't yet earned the money. If for some reason your kid doesn't earn at least $2,000, you can either withdraw the excess or recharacterize it as a contribution for a future year. There will be no taxes or penalties, as long as you make the adjustment within the allotted time frame (see IRS publication 590, *Individual Retirement Arrangements*).

The results of this head start can be astounding, especially when applied to a child's extended investment horizon. If you have a fifteen-year-old and you make a $2,000 annual contribution to her Roth IRA at the end of each of the next four years, she will have $1,089,622 when she turns sixty-eight, assuming a 10% annual return. But make those contributions at the *beginning* of each year, and she will have $1,198,584 at age sixty-eight, an extra amount of $108,962!

Regardless of when you can make the contributions, don't let any of your child's legitimate earnings go by without considering them as the basis for a Roth IRA contribution. For every eligible dollar in earnings you neglect to deposit into a Roth IRA, your child will lose $117 in tax-free retirement dollars, assuming the dollar would have had a 10% average annual rate of return for fifty years.

Skip four years of $2,000 contributions, and your kid could miss out on over $1,000,000 of federally tax-free money at her retirement! It's going to be hard enough to get her to visit you in the nursing home. Don't give her a million more reasons to avoid you.

2. Investment Method You can use stocks, bonds, or certificates of deposit as the investment vehicle, but you will find the easiest and most flexible option will initially be a mutual fund (see Chapter 1). However, not every mutual fund company will establish a Roth IRA for a minor. Because relatively few people are contributing to a Roth IRA for a child (apparently some people just don't care about their children's futures as much as you do), some fund companies have not yet formed the legal mechanisms necessary to maintain custody of these types of accounts.

But at the time this book was published, the following fund companies allowed parents to open a Roth IRA for a child with legitimate earned income:

Fund company	Telephone number
Alliance Capital Management	1-800-221-5672
American Century Investments	1-800-345-2021
American Express	1-800-297-7378
American Funds	1-800-421-9900
Evergreen Funds	1-800-343-2898
Franklin/Templeton Funds	1-800-632-2301
Gabelli Funds	1-800-422-3554
Heritage Family of Funds	1-800-421-4184
IDEX	1-800-851-9777
Invesco	1-800-525-8085
Janus Group	1-800-525-8983
Legg Mason	1-800-577-8589
Lord Abbett	1-800-426-1130
MFS Family of Funds	1-800-225-2606
Prudential	1-800-225-6292
SchwabFunds	1-800-225-8570
Scudder Funds	1-800-621-1048
Stein Roe	1-800-338-2550
Strong Funds	1-800-368-1030
T. Rowe Price	1-800-638-5660
TIAA-CREF Mutual Funds	1-800-223-1200
USAA Group	1-800-382-8722
Van Kampen	1-800-341-2911
Vanguard	1-800-662-7447

One factor you should consider when deciding which fund company to use is what type of investment philosophy you (and eventually your child) will adopt. You can afford to be relatively aggressive with your child's Roth IRA (I said "aggressive," not "reckless"). Your child will have at least four or five decades until she can gain access to this money without a penalty, so short-term downturns now probably won't have a lasting affect on her retirement comfort level. And if your willingness to accept some volatility in the value of her Roth IRA allows you to earn even 1% more per year on average, the results can be staggering.

Say your child works from the ages of fifteen to eighteen, and earns at least $2,000 in each of those four years, and you make corresponding deposits into a Roth IRA. Look at the difference in the amount of money she will have at the age of sixty-eight, depending on whether she earns a 9%, 10%, or 11% annual average rate of return:

Average Annual Rate of Return	Amount at Age 68
9%	$ 690,186
10%	1,089,621
11%	1,713,130

Over $1 million difference between 9% and 11%! This is not only a great illustration as to why you need to maximize your rate of return, but it also shows why you should pay close attention to funds with low annual expenses.

3. Contributions You can make the annual Roth IRA contributions or your child can, up to $2,000 in 2001, $3,000 for 2002–2004, $4,000 for 2005–2007, and $5,000 in 2008. If you want her to contribute her money to the account, you should tell her why, and how much you expect her to put in.

But don't be surprised if she shows little or no interest in contributing to her retirement account with her hard-earned paycheck. I didn't when I was her age, and you probably didn't either. You may want to offer to match each of her contributions at a rate that you can afford—say, two dollars for each one she puts in. If she is willing to do this, she is still head and shoulders above her peer group, and has a solid long-term financial perspective.

Finally, if she refuses to put any money at all into the account, use your own money. This is perfectly legal as long as you don't exceed her earnings and you stay under the annual limit. Chalk it up to one more thing that parents do for children, even if the kids don't appreciate it until later in life. Keep in mind, though, that if you do put your own money in her Roth IRA, it becomes her money, and she can do whatever she wants with it when she reaches adulthood.

4. Teaching Your Child Even if your kid won't use her own money to contribute to her Roth IRA, you should still make your best effort to include her in the process of establishing and maintaining the account. Not only will this be a great opportunity to teach her about investing, you will find she is more likely to contribute her own money to the account if she understands why it is so important that she make this sacrifice now. Help her learn about different investment options, and let her make some decisions once she has done her research.

Don't be discouraged if she doesn't show a lot of interest initially. As time goes by, three things will happen. She will grow older, the amount of money will grow larger, and eventually she won't be able to ignore the account.

The Big Reward—Withdrawing the Money

The great advantage to the Roth IRA becomes apparent when your kid starts taking the money out. The pittance she paid in extra taxes by using a Roth IRA (instead of a deductible one) will have been long forgotten. But those few dollars sacrificed eons ago have by now saved your child hundreds of thousands of dollars in taxes. Assuming your child is in a 31% tax bracket at retirement, $1 million in a Roth IRA is equal to $1,449,275 in a regular IRA, 401(k) plan, or tax-deferred variable annuity, on an after-tax basis.

What's more, the Roth IRA does not have a mandatory distribution schedule, so your child will have considerably more withdrawal flexibility with a Roth than with other types of retirement accounts.

But just because the Roth IRA is a great retirement planning vehicle, that doesn't mean your child won't be able to get at the money for other important expenditures during her life. The IRS allows access to the Roth IRA before age 59½ for the following purposes:

1. College Tuition Under today's rules, most financial aid offices will not consider a child's retirement plan as an asset available to pay for college. Consequently, the Roth IRA shouldn't hurt your child's financial aid eligibility.

However, she can still use the money to pay for college. She can always withdraw the *contributions* with no taxes or penalty. And as long as the earnings are used for higher education expenses, there will be no 10% penalty on withdrawing the gains in the account. She will, however, pay *taxes* on the earnings, albeit at her lower rate.

2. The House Down Payment A Roth IRA can be tapped tax-free for a first-time home purchase (for tax purposes, "first-time" means that your child has not been the primary owner of a residence for at least two years). There is a $10,000 lifetime limit to the amount that can be withdrawn.

Although your child can use the Roth IRA to help pay for these nonretirement expenditures, the cost of doing so can be enormous. If your child withdraws $10,000 to pay for college or a house, it will cost her $1,173,908 fifty years after the withdrawal, assuming the money would have earned 10% annually.

So the Roth IRA should only be used as a last-resort source of funds.

Getting Started

You don't get many chances to *cost* your kid millions of dollars, but that's what failing to use her earnings to open a Roth IRA might do. There really is no other investment that can turn so few dollars today into such monstrous after-tax dollars for use in your child's retirement.

The following IRS publications will help you navigate the tax and paperwork complexities of a working teenager (none of them contains the secret to getting a kid out of bed at dark-thirty A.M. to deliver newspapers). They can be found at your local IRS office, by calling 1-800-829-1040, or by visiting www.irs.gov.

Publication 4	*Student's Guide to Federal Income Tax*
Publication 533	*Self-Employment Tax*
Publication 583	*Starting a Business and Keeping Records*
Publication 929	*Tax Rules for Children and Dependents*

chapter nine

Giving Your Kid a Well-Timed Nudge into His 401(k)

Having a Mutually Rewarding Discussion When Your Child Gets a "Real" Job

In 2001, one of the greatest wealth creators in history turned twenty years old. I'm not talking about Britney Spears or some dot-com entrepreneur. Instead, I'm speaking of the retirement plan that came to be known by the legislative subsection that unleashed this omnipresent saving tool: the 401(k). Americans now have over $2 trillion of their net worth sitting in their work-sponsored retirement accounts.

Most of us now know how powerful these plans can be, but very few of us began contributing the minute we were first eligible. When you started working, you probably knew it was something you should do, but you were fresh out of school, working for peanuts, and looking to buy a house and start a family. Or you just had to have that 1986 Camaro IROC (heaven help you if you are still lusting after that car). Retirement was a distant concept compared to these more pressing needs.

Eventually you got a little older and a little wiser. Maybe someone you respected at work prodded you into beginning to save a little each paycheck. Or you realized how important the employer match was, and decided to sacrifice some current desires to at least get your company's contribution. By the time you were in your thirties, you were glad you had started contributing, but you were kicking yourself for not beginning sooner (see "Ten Things You Need to Know," #2, page 39).

How much did your delay actually cost you? And what can you do to help your kid avoid the mistakes you made?

Your child's first exposure to a retirement plan at work is a crucial point in his becoming financially independent. Of course, his 401(k) will eventually represent the lion's share of his wealth, and will likely be his main source of support when he stops working. But it is also important in that it may be his first exposure to investing as an adult, and might be the motivation to convert him from a spender to a saver. And it could be the only time in his life where his paycheck isn't wiped out with other big obligations, like a mortgage payment or grocery bill.

Yet, as great as the opportunity is for your child's first 401(k) enrollment to launch him on the road to becoming a millionaire, getting him started is not as easy as just filling out a few forms. According to a study done by the Employee Benefit Research Institute, over two-thirds of employees between the ages of twenty-one and twenty-four don't participate in a work-sponsored retirement plan. And almost half of all workers between the ages of eighteen and thirty-four don't contribute to a plan, either.

Even if your child wants to learn the best ways to maximize his retirement plan options, help may be difficult to find. A study conducted by the Spectrem Group showed that only 16% of 401(k) participants had access to investment advice. His company probably won't provide much in the way of personalized help, and neither will the plan provider. Unless your family already has a willing financial adviser, your child's relatively meager assets will make it hard for him to get outside assistance.

That's where you come in. Ultimately the responsibility to enroll, contribute, and manage his plan will fall on your child's shoulders. But when your child starts his first "real" job, you are likely to be a VIP for advice on his 401(k).

This time can be a tremendous opportunity for both of you, beyond just dollars and cents. He is probably going to be a little intimidated by the thick packet of retirement plan enrollment forms plopped in his "in" box. By gently offering to sit down with him and go through the paperwork, you relieve him of the burden of having to ask for your help. And once you begin going over the information, you will find yourselves talking about other issues that you might have never addressed; things like money, work, and balancing priorities.

You might be hesitant to initiate a conversation about your kid's 401(k), as you might be in the dark about some things in your *own* retirement plan. Don't worry. You can take comfort in the fact that you probably know more than your child does. And you can use the following tips to help him get started, keep going, and avoid potential hazards along the way.

1. Start Early You can see the importance of beginning as soon as possible in the following example. When people see this demonstration for the first time, they usually react the same way. Their jaws drop, their faces go white with disbelief, and speech becomes difficult. Eventually, they regain their composure and accuse me of lying or using witchcraft to achieve these results.

Joe and Beth are both twenty-two. They work at the same company and earn the same salary. Their benevolent employer matches employee contributions at a rate of twenty-five cents on the dollar (that is, for each dollar the employee puts into the plan, the employer contributes twenty-five cents).

Joe decides to contribute to the plan from the day he starts working. He has to sacrifice a bit, and maybe he can't afford to buy the nicest possible car or purchase a house right away. But he thinks he'll be able to do those things some day, and for right now he wants to get that employer match.

If your child wants to contribute to his plan but feels as though he can't afford to, the two of you can go through the Painful, Powerful Prioritization process described in the Introduction of this book. This exercise will give your child an opportunity to learn more about the concepts of budgeting and saving, and add to the "financial foundation" that will guide his money decisions for the rest of his life.

He plans on contributing $4,000 per year (about $150 every two weeks) and then will get an employer match of $1,000 annually. He vows to do this for ten years, then stop contributing and start looking for a house.

Beth sees things differently. Her salary represents the first "real" money she has ever had, and she intends to enjoy it. She buys a nice car, and rents a luxury apartment in a great neighborhood. She plans to contribute to her retirement plan, but figures even if she waits ten years to start, she'll still be able to contribute from the age of 32 until she retires at 65.

So how do they fare? Beth contributes $4,000 every year from age 32 until she turns 65. If the account averages a 10% annual rate of return, with the employer match it will look something like this:

Beth's Contribution	Company Match	Total at Age 65
$172,000	$43,000	$1,111,257

Not bad at all. Let's see how this compares to Joe. Remember, he is only going to contribute from age 22 to 32, or ten years. At the same 10% annualized rate of return, his account will look like this:

Joe's Contribution	Company Match	Total at Age 65
$40,000	$10,000	$1,850,745

You read it right. Even though I have done this calculation a few hundred different times, I always have to double-check my numbers because the results are so astounding. Joe has over $700,000 more than Beth, even though the contributions for Joe's account amounted to less than one fourth of what went into Beth's account. And for the sake of my example, I had Joe quit contributing to this account at the age of thirty-two!

What's the explanation for the huge difference between the two workers? No magic. It's just that by the time Beth even starts contributing, Joe has accumulated $79,687. If Beth insists on waiting until she turns thirty-two, she would be required to have over $8,300 put in her account annually over the next thirty-three years just to equal the amount of money Joe gets for ten years of contributions.

And although Joe could have stopped contributing to pop for a few other things, and still been far ahead of Beth when they compared accounts at the Senior Center, my experience is that early starters to a retirement plan never stop contributing. If Joe's a smart guy and keeps dropping his deposits in, he will be looking at almost $3 million by the time he turns sixty-five.

And if Joe is like most workers his income (and deposits) will rise over his career. Raising his biweekly contribution by 5% each year will give Joe a retirement account balance approaching the *eight-figure* range by the time he's in his seventies. This example should be required reading for every American worker, and it is electrifying proof of "Ten Things You Need to Know," #2 (see page 39).

2. The Match If there is a kid you care about who is just beginning his career, show him the above example. And while you're at it, ask him if his new employer matches any contributions and at what rate. If he is fortunate enough to be working at such a company, you can also tell him that this match is probably the one and only instantaneous, guaranteed investment he may ever have.

This concept might seem pretty obvious to you and me, but

you would be surprised how many new workers don't appreciate the magnitude of this situation. When you sit down with
him, tell him about the miracle of putting a dollar into a retirement plan (where it remains his *own* money), and immediately
getting a guaranteed return in the amount of the match on that
dollar, assuming he remains with his employer long enough to
become vested. Point out that he will never, ever get an opportunity to make this type of automatic profit anywhere else
in his life. Do not let up until he agrees to begin contributing to
the plan, at least enough to get all the matching funds from his
employer.

If that doesn't work, you are going to have to result to a
more sordid tactic: bribery. Tell him you will match any contributions he makes to the plan in cash (you might want to use
any money that you saved in your own name and intended
eventually to give to him).

At the end of each year, have him show you his statement
from his company's plan. You can give him whatever match
you feel comfortable with, whether it is dollar-for-dollar, 50
cents, whatever. Maybe put a declining percentage of your
match to reflect the importance of starting early. Something like
this might be effective:

Year	Your Match
1	100%
2	90
3	80
4	70
5	60

Keep after him each year to see his statement. Write him a
check for the amount of his contribution, minus any loans or
withdrawals he has taken from the plan, and tell him he can
spend it on whatever he wants. My guess is, however, that
eventually he'll realize he can live without the money that has

been going into his 401(k) and will either invest your check or tell you to keep it (these kinds of moments make me get all weepy).

This enticement accomplishes your goal of getting him started early, yet he doesn't have to give up very much in spending money to start building his retirement plan. And for your few thousand dollars of bribery, you can make a huge difference in the ending value of your child's retirement plan.

Let's apply the bribery technique to Joe's and Beth's employer match and investment schedule. If you were using this method to encourage Beth to start her retirement plan today, it would have cost you the following amount (based on your matching 50 cents for each dollar at the aforementioned declining schedule, and Beth agreeing to contribute $4,000 per year):

Year	Your Check to Beth
1	$2,000
2	1,800
3	1,600
4	1,400
5	1,200
Total	$8,000

Assuming the employer matches at a 25% rate, and Beth's account earns 10% per year, by the time Beth reaches sixty-five your five-year matching strategy would give her an extra $1,141,786 in her 401(k)! You turned your $8,000 bribe into well over a million dollars.

3. No 401(k)? IRA! Some companies either don't offer a retirement plan, or require new hires to work at their job for a year before they are eligible to contribute to the company plan. If your child is in this situation, don't let him off the hook. Instead, encourage him to open a self-directed IRA account at a mutual fund or brokerage firm. One $3,000 deposit at 10% annually would be worth \$218,671 forty-five years later, plus he will lower his current income tax bill by close to a thousand dollars. Better yet, have him make a Roth IRA contribution instead (see Chapter 8). He won't get the current tax deduction, but he may save hundreds of thousands of dollars in federal taxes on the withdrawals when he retires.

The tax law changes in 2001 created a great opportunity for lower-income taxpayers to make IRA or Roth IRA contributions *and* cut their taxes. Basically, your nonstudent, nondependent child with income under \$15,000 (\$30,000 if married filing jointly) gets 50 cents in taxes refunded for each dollar put into either type of IRA, up to \$1,000. This credit is phased out at \$25,000 (\$50,000 if married filing jointly) and is scheduled to disappear in 2006. Give your poor child \$2,000 for his IRA, and he will get a \$1,000 tax refund from the government!

---

4. Asset Allocation Once your child agrees to participate in his retirement plan at work, his next question will be, "Which investment options should I use?"

Your answer should be something along the lines of, "Whatever will make you the most money." To which he will roll his eyes.

Most workers in their twenties have around 75% of their retirement plan balances in equities. But you can make the argument that your child's allocation should not only be 100% in equities, but it should be tilted heavily toward smaller companies that have more volatility, yet also a higher potential for growth.

The reason for this is threefold. First of all, he won't be able to touch this money without a penalty for around forty years. Second, his paycheck contributions will act as a dollar-cost averaging program (see Chapter 1), buying more shares during downturns and fewer at the peaks. Finally, his account balance will be relatively small for years to come, so any potential pull-backs won't have a material loss in terms of actual dollars.

The benefit to earning a slightly higher average annual re-turn can be astounding over your child's forty- or fifty-year time horizon. Compare what $4,000 invested annually over forty-five years amounts to at different annual rates of return:

Annual Return	Ending Balance
8%	$1,546,022
10%	2,875,619
12%	5,432,920

Four percent more per year means over 3½ times as much money at retirement!

5. Rebalancing If your child does choose to diversify his retire-ment portfolio among different types of stock and bond funds, you can help him smooth out the highs and lows of his account totals by teaching him to rebalance his account on a regular basis. "Rebalancing" means adjusting the current makeup of a portfolio so that the percentages in each fund are equal to the desired ratio—such as 60% stocks, 30% bonds, and 10% cash. Kind of like driving a car—if you drift too far toward the center of the road or the shoulder, you have to correct your steering to stay in your lane.

Many investors who deposited their retirement plan dollars into technology-based stock mutual funds during the late 1990s were rewarded with astounding returns over a very short period of time. Gains of 50% to 100% previously took years to achieve, but during this era even neophyte shareholders were seeing their retirement assets double in a matter of months.

This performance caused a shift in the makeup of investors' retirement plans. Participants who started with a moderate mix of say, 60% stocks, 30% bonds, and 10% in a money market, might have ended a big year with 85% stocks, 10% bonds, and 5% in a money market, even though they didn't change a thing in the blend of their assets.

Confronted with this new portfolio breakdown, most investors continued to do nothing. Or, worse yet, they wondered aloud why they had any money at all in boring bonds or cash, when everybody knew the real money was to be made in stocks. After reaching this epiphany, they dialed their plan's toll-free customer service number, changed their personal asset allocation to 100% stocks, and began to dream of retiring ten or fifteen years earlier than they had originally planned.

But like all great parties, the NASDAQ celebration came to an end (I think it was the same day an eighty-eight-year-old widow asked me what I knew about "Crisco" Systems. I think she meant "Cisco."). The plunge in technology stocks that began in March 2000 taught some people a valuable lesson in "return math": A 100% gain, followed by a 50% loss, puts you right back to where you started. And the hangover was particularly severe for people who let huge initial gains in their stock funds throw their asset allocation model out of whack.

Yet if investors had rebalanced their portfolios each year to their original asset mix, there is a good chance they could have avoided much of the pain of the bear market of 2000 and 2001. Say a retirement account had three investment options: stocks, bonds, and a money market. And the hypothetical return of each account over three years looked like this:

	Year 1	Year 2	Year 3
Stocks	+50%	−30%	+10%
Bonds	−10	+20	+6
Cash	+5	+4	+4

If an investor had started this period with $100,000 spread among these three accounts in a 70/20/10 mix, and never rebalanced the accounts, at the end of the three years he would have

$115,103, for an average annual rate of return of about 4.8%. But if he had returned his portfolio to his original 70/20/10 asset allocation at the end of each year, his three-year ride through the volatility would have left him with $120,914 (almost $6,000 more), for an annualized return rate of about 6.6%.

There are two things that might prevent your child from using this strategy effectively. The first obstacle is that it requires him to sell a portion of an investment that has done well, and use the proceeds to buy more of an investment that has done poorly. This is like grounding a child for a straight-A report card, while taking another kid with Ds and Fs out to dinner. But the rebalancing strategy forces an investor to practice a philosophy that has made money for thousands of years: buying low, and selling high.

The second reason the benefits of this strategy could elude your child is that he might agree with the philosophy, but he might neglect to put his thoughts into action.

Some plans offer "lifestyle" funds, which not only allocate the assets according to a predetermined model but also rebalance the portfolio when it gets out of whack. Not a bad way to go— less hassle for your kid, and you don't even have to explain what "rebalance" means!

Tell him to pick one day each year to check the dollar amount of each account, and to rebalance accordingly. Anything more than this will be overkill, and anything less will make it difficult to keep doing regularly. I've always recommended that people use their birthday as the day to check their portfolio percentages, because it's easy to remember. But if it were up to me, we would add the day to the sillier holidays already on the calendar. I think we'll all be better off when Hallmark comes out with a "Happy Portfolio Rebalancing Day" line of greeting cards.

6. Owning a Piece of the Action One retirement plan investment option your child may be offered is the chance to buy
stock in his employer. This can be attractive to a young employee, as he probably has an optimistic view of his company's
future (after all, they were smart enough to hire *him*, weren't
they?). He wants to help the company grow, and participate in
the long-term rewards of his efforts. The company might encourage him to buy the stock by offering shares at a discount, or
matching his contributions with shares of stock.

There is a tax loophole in using company stock that employees can exploit to reduce the taxation of withdrawals from a retirement account. Normally, any distributions your child takes
from the account in retirement are taxed as ordinary income.
But if your child has individual shares in his qualified plan, he
can "roll" the shares out of the plan, and pay income taxes only
on his employer's cost basis of the shares.

Once he sells the shares, he pays capital gains taxes on any
profits he has made. Under 2001 tax rates, this could be the difference between paying almost 40% income tax, versus as little
as 8% long-term capital gains tax. For someone who worked for
Wal-Mart over the last thirty years, the tax savings could be
hundreds of thousands of dollars.

But employee ownership and tax benefits aside, your child
may want to keep his company stock to just a small portion of
his retirement plan. He already is depending on his employer
for his income; any protracted downturn in the company's for-
tunes could mean a cut in pay for him, or he could even be laid
off. If this happens while he has a majority of his assets in the
company's stock, his long-term investments may look as dis-
mal as his short-term employment situation. Talk about too
many eggs in one basket.

7. It's a Retirement Plan, Not a Bank After your child has con-
tributed to his retirement plan for a few years, he will probably
be pleasantly surprised at the amount of money he has accu-

mulated. But if his plan has a loan provision, this tidy sum can become a tempting source of quick cash. In the best scenario, borrowing from a 401(k) is a bad idea. In the worst case, it can generate a huge tax bill when your child can least afford it, and cost him a fortune at retirement.

Borrowing from the plan seems like an innocent transaction. After all, there's no credit check, no collateral required, and your child is paying himself back, with interest. But the dollars that went into the plan initially were from his pretax income, while the loan repayments come from after-tax dollars. If your child earns $20 per hour, he needs fifty hours of work to generate a $1,000 deposit into his 401(k). But he would need about eighty-four hours of work at the same wage to pay back $1,000 borrowed from the plan (and that doesn't include any interest charged).

The situation becomes especially dire if he loses his job while he has an outstanding retirement plan loan. A majority of plans require employees to repay any loans immediately upon termination. Unless he has cash set aside (unlikely, since if he did, then he wouldn't have to borrow the money in the first place!), he won't be able to pay the loan off. The outstanding balance will then be treated as an early distribution, and he will owe state and federal taxes, plus a 10% penalty.

Taxes and penalties usually total about half of whatever the distribution is. If a twenty-five-year-old worker takes a $10,000 loan from his plan, then loses his job and can't repay the loan, the effect on his retirement account at age sixty-five would look like this (assuming a 10% annual return):

	What It Would Have Been Worth at Age 65
Loan amount ($10,000)	$452,592
Taxes and penalties ($5,000)	226,296
Total deficit at retirement	$678,888

Almost $700,000 less at retirement, all for a loan less than the price of a decent used car. Other than needing a new kidney, I can't think of a reason why your child should consider borrowing from his retirement plan. He is much better off going first to a bank, and then to you. If he can't get any money from the first two options, he should reconsider just how urgently he needs the money.

8. Roll It Over, Not Out The example above shows what a terrible effect a premature withdrawal from a 401(k) can have on your child's financial future. Yet when many twenty-somethings leave their first full-time job, they opt to take the cash out of their retirement plan. A report from Fidelity Investments showed that about one out of three terminated employees with plan balances under $10,000 took the check, rather than rolling the money over to another qualified plan.

Sometimes they do this because they need the money, but my experience has been that, more likely, the paperwork is too complicated. If your kid changes jobs, make sure he either rolls his retirement account over into a new employer's plan or establishes a self-directed IRA. If a few minutes of your time will ensure he doesn't withdraw the money, you might have saved him hundreds of thousands of dollars at retirement.

And when your child *does* roll the money over into an IRA, he doesn't necessarily have to liquidate the shares and start over (possibly incurring new sales charges and fees). Tell him he can choose to have the funds rolled over "in kind," meaning that his portfolio will be sent intact to a self-directed IRA.

The tax law package of 2001 mandated that, unless notified otherwise by the employee, retirement plan providers must automatically recharacterize the 401(k) plans of separating employees into IRAs, as long as the balances are between $1,000 and $5,000.

Getting Started

When your child starts his first full-time job, offer to sit down with him to go over his retirement plan options. You can get objective analysis of the funds offered through www.morningstar.com, and you can find more information about work-sponsored retirement plans at www.mpower.com.

A few minutes of your time and some of your wisdom might mean hundreds of thousands more for him at his retirement. And you get a bonus, too. By hearing about what you know, and what you've learned over your decades as a worker and an investor, he might realize that despite what he thought during his teenage years, you really aren't an idiot.

PART FOUR

Into Adulthood

Whew. College should be just about over by now, unless your child is heading off to grad, law, or med school (if so, you have my congratulations and pity at the same time!).

If she is working, make sure she is salting money away in that retirement plan at work! And speaking of retirement plans, you are probably making yours now (if not *living* them). This might crimp how much you can actually do for your child, but hopefully the steps you took for her way back when are really starting to add up.

Your child might be getting ready to make one of the most exciting *tangible* investments she will ever make: buying her first house. This should be fun for you and her, and even if this is a time of tight cash for you, you have a bunch of ways to make this purchase smart and easy.

One (good) problem you might be facing in regard to

your own money is the size of your assets. You are probably near your peak earning years, with a highly appreciated (and almost debt-free) house, and your dependents won't be depending on your income for long. Add things up, and there might be enough that you are considered "rich," at least in the eyes of the IRS. Estate taxes could be a danger to your family's future, so an hour or two examining your options could be worth hundreds of thousands of dollars in taxes avoided.

chapter ten

A Million-Dollar Roof Over Her Head

Helping Your Child Purchase a Home

The financial picture of the typical American is changing. The growing prevalence of stocks, bonds, and retirement accounts is shrinking the "home equity" portion of our net worth.

But that's no reason to overlook helping your adult child buy a house as a great way to give her financial independence. She has to live somewhere, and although in some cases renting may be her smartest choice for the time being, home ownership can provide her with shelter *and* can be an extremely compelling long-term investment.

By the time Rachel and I decided to buy a house, I had been a financial adviser for over a decade. I handled my father's investments, and we joked about his ignorance of all things monetary. But over the years he had bought homes four times, which was exactly four more home transactions than I had been involved in. Add his ownership and maintenance experience to the fact that I can barely change a lightbulb without a trip to the emergency room, and you can bet we appreciated his assistance as we began our search!

Your child may want to go through the ups and downs of her first home purchase on her own, and that's okay. But if she is willing to listen to you, your knowledge and experience can be priceless to her, especially since all the well-intentioned real estate agents, appraisers, and bankers she will talk to might have an inherent conflict of interest that will cloud their advice.

And, like a lot of parents, you may choose this opportunity to subsidize her home purchase with a little (or a lot) of your money. But before you decide if this is the best destination for your dollars, it will help if you understand the bottom-line economic reality of home ownership, and how it compares to other investment options.

Building Wealth Through Home Ownership

The most obvious force driving the investment aspect of owning a home is that since the end of World War II, home prices have generally risen, and that trend shows no signs of letting up.

Although every region goes through boom-and-bust housing markets, only a fool would bet against a trend as powerful as the upward movement in home values. And if history keeps repeating itself like this, your child will not only enjoy the benefit of borrowing money to buy an appreciating asset, but will also experience the miracle of owning a house that is increasing in value while the loan payment stays the same.

1. Borrowing to Buy an Appreciating Asset The power of "leverage" is easiest to demonstrate with an example of your child purchasing a $150,000 house (this is a little above the median home sales price, according to the National Realtors Association). Banks are willing to loan her most of the purchase price—say, 90% of the value. This means she only has to pay 10% down ($15,000) to get an asset worth $150,000. Let's say she takes a 30-year mortgage with an interest rate at 8%, and the home appreciates in value at a rate of 4% per year over three years. What would the net gain on her $15,000 investment be after three years?

Well, ignoring the issues of taxes, interest deductibility, and selling commissions, and assuming her mortgage payment equaled what she would have paid in rent, her home would be worth $168,729, meaning she now has $37,400 of equity versus her original $15,000. This translates into a remarkable annualized growth rate in her equity of about 35%, and it probably happened before she was able to unpack!

As time goes by, she will continue to pay down her mortgage. This reduces her leverage as her equity builds. But after fifteen years of 4% annual price appreciation, her equity will still have grown at an annualized rate of 17%.

2. Rising Value, Steady Payments The second inflationary advantage to home ownership occurs when your child purchases a home using a fixed mortgage. When she purchases a $150,000 home with 10% down and an 8% thirty-year mortgage, her total annual mortgage payments would be around $11,880 (about 8% of the value of the house). Assuming again a 4% average annual rise in the value of the home, after ten years the value would be about $222,000. But her annual mortgage payments are still only $11,880, about 5% of the value of the house. If the trend continues for thirty years, her annual mortgage payments are only 2.4% of a $486,509 home.

Put another way, assuming an annual overall inflation rate of 3%, after thirty years her $990 monthly mortgage payment is equal to only $408 in today's dollars! The mortgage will seem like peanuts by then, barely a bill worth noticing, whereas if she keeps on renting, her landlord is going to jack up her rent at least as fast as her building grows in value.

3. A Real-Life Example So the investment aspects of home ownership will likely be favorable to your child over the long run. But is it realistic to think that the average homeowner today could become a millionaire? Well, yes, especially if you consider the recent enactment of the exclusion from taxation of up to $500,000 in capital gains on a house for married couples

($250,000 for single people, or married people filing separately).

Say your daughter is twenty-eight years old. She is recently married, and after consulting with you, she and her husband have decided to purchase a $150,000 home. But they need your help with a down payment to get started. Between their savings and your gift, they have $30,000 for the down payment. They take a thirty-year mortgage at 8%.

Consider the following hypothetical factors for the next twenty-eight years:

• Their houses appreciate in value at a rate of 4% per year.

• They move every seven years (about average for Americans), each time buying a house that costs 20% more than the one they're selling.

• Each time they buy a new house, they take out a 15-year mortgage at 8%, applying the equity from their previous house against the price of the new house.

• They pay a 6% commission every time they sell a house.

• Within the next three decades, the capital gains exclusion is eventually adjusted upward for inflation (a commonsense notion, yet we can only hope), to an amount over $750,000 for a married couple.

By the time twenty-eight years have gone by, your daughter and her husband have no more children at home, and are ready to sell their house to move into a smaller, more appropriate one. They are able to sell it for about $730,000 after the real estate agent's commission. When they pay off the outstanding mortgage, their remaining amount looks like this:

Net sales proceeds	$730,000
Less outstanding loan	–173,000
Net amount	$557,000

They use this money to pay cash for a low-maintenance condominium. It also appreciates at a rate of 4% over the next seven years. At this point, your daughter and her husband are both sixty-three years old, and decide to retire. They sell the condominium so they can travel the world together. After the agent's commission, they net out about $700,000.

A nice amount, to be sure. But it's not a million dollars. Yet if we factor in the tax-free status of the gains your daughter has made and then compare it to the after-tax value of other investments, the actual worth becomes apparent.

Assume when your daughter is sixty-three years old, her income tax bracket is 36% at the federal level and 7% at the state. She pays 10% federal tax on long-term capital gains and 5% at the state level. She and her husband would need the following amounts in these other investment vehicles to receive the same after-tax amounts of $700,000:

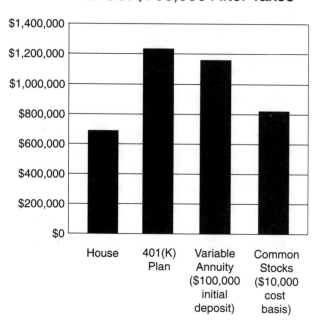

Example of Value Needed to Get $700,000 After Taxes*

* Assuming capital gains from the sale of the house are excluded from taxation.

This is pretty impressive, especially considering that your daughter's mortgage payment would never be higher than $1,200 in today's dollars (at 3% inflation). And the money spent on the house payment was not discretionary—whether owning or renting, they would always have some form of monthly housing cost.

If your daughter and her husband decide not to keep up with the Joneses and stay in their original house for the entire thirty-five years, the results are even more impressive. Let's say they pay off their original mortgage in fifteen years. They have been living without that money for all those years, and so rather than spending it, they decide to start depositing the amount previously used to pay their mortgage into a mutual fund (see Chapter 1). By the time they are sixty-three years old their house and account values are as follows:

Home value	$ 592,000
Mutual fund (10% annual rate of return)	871,000
Total worth	$1,463,000

Is Now the Right Time?

These extraordinary examples are tangible proof of the wealth creation generated by owning a home, and will only kindle your excitement about the idea of your child's buying a house, especially if she is in her late twenties or early thirties.

But sometimes parents' experience in the positive financial aspects of home ownership can cause them to be a little too enthusiastic in recommending that a child purchase a house as soon as possible. If you are guilty of this, you can't really be blamed. You only want what is best for your child, and you would like her to benefit from being a homeowner in the same way you probably have.

However, the changing nature of the way we live and work has made first-time home buying a different ballgame than it was twenty or thirty years ago. When my parents were in their early twenties (about 1966) it was not uncommon for people to get a job fresh out of college or high school, and then work for the same company for thirty years or more, living in the same town. Once people bought a home in a community, there was a reasonable amount of certainty that they would stay in that house for the coming decades.

My neighborhood is proof of the way things were. I live in the same area in which I grew up. Many of the people who lived near me when I was a child are, once again, my neighbors (and although they are thirty years older than me, they've aged much better than I have).

The future of today's twenty-somethings is not quite so predictable. People are not only less likely to work for the same company for their adult lives, they may even switch careers three or four times during the duration of their employment.

The metropolitan areas that are currently attracting many young workers (Silicon Valley; Seattle; Boston; Austin, Texas) have seen a corresponding escalation in home prices. This booming atmosphere causes a double dose of anxiety for prospective first-time home purchasers. The rapidly rising prices make them desperate to get into a house as soon as possible, yet they are rightfully afraid of buying at the peak of the local economic cycle. If they do make that mistake, they end up overpaying for a home that they soon may not be able to afford if they are "downsized."

Even if young adults are able keep their jobs during a downturn, buying a home in a hot geographic location can sometimes mean years of being "underwater" (owing more on the house than they can readily sell it for). According to the National Association of Realtors, home prices in the Los Angeles area rose only 4% in the *five years* between 1992 and 1997 (compared to Salt Lake City, where home prices almost doubled in the same period). Even in a relatively stable market, it can take about four years of ownership before a buyer breaks even on a purchase, once loan costs, real estate commissions, and moving expenses are included.

The fact that people are choosing to marry later in life may also have an effect on the timing of your child's first home purchase. If she plans on getting married, it may be smarter for her to rent until she knows that she and her future spouse can find suitable employment in the same community (if they have to move, selling a house soon after buying it can be an expensive proposition).

Yet, if the other variables are in place, don't discourage your child from buying a house just because she is single. According to the Census Bureau, 23.2% of unmarried people ages twenty-three to thirty-four owned homes in 1998—the highest number ever for that particular demographic group.

A good rule of thumb is that the larger the city she lives in, the better it is for your child to delay the purchase of a first-time home. This is especially true if she already has a safe, comfortable, and affordable place to rent for the time being.

Helping Your Child Without Spending Any of Your Own Money

It is not uncommon for parents to want to contribute money to a child's first home purchase. Many of us remember how hard it was to scrape together enough money to buy a home, when we were also starting our families. If you decide not to help your child out of principle, then that is your right as a parent. But if you think you can't help her financially because you don't have enough money, then you haven't been exposed to all the different ways your dollars can help your child, whether it's a few hundred or a few hundred thousand.

Getting a Loan

However, before you decide if (and how much) you want to contribute financially, there are several things you can do to help her get a loan and buy the house that's right for her. And none of these approaches requires you to open your pocketbook.

The most important nonfinancial way you can help your child decide how much house she can afford is by pointing out the financial ratios bankers use when deciding how large a mortgage she can get. Almost all lending institutions use the following percentages of overall monthly income to decide how much house your child's income will buy, and how the mortgage payment will fit with your child's other monthly debt payments:

Mortgage + taxes + insurance	**No more than 28% of gross monthly income**
Above + all debt service payments	**No more than 36% of gross monthly income**

These numbers can be very sobering to an enthusiastic young home buyer, especially if there is only one income on which to base the numbers. Take a typical financial situation of a relatively successful young person:

Monthly salary	**$3,500**
Car payment	300
Student loan payment	200

Twenty-eight percent of $3,500 is $980, and figuring $200 in taxes and $75 in insurance leaves a mortgage payment of $705. A thirty-year fixed mortgage at 8% would mean that your child could afford a maximum loan of $96,079. The actual value of the home your child can purchase depends on the size of the down payment she can make, but if she has less than 20% of the home's purchase price, her banker may require her to take out private mortgage insurance until the loan balance is less than 80% of the house's value. This additional monthly expense will further reduce the maximum mortgage allowed.

The situation becomes even gloomier when the total "debt service ratio" (the amount of money that your child is using to pay off any and all loans) is calculated. Thirty-six percent of $3,500 is $1,260. Subtracting the car and student loan payments means there is $760 for the mortgage, taxes, and insurance. Estimating $175 for taxes and $50 for insurance leaves only $535. Taking the same thirty-year 8% mortgage, your child can now borrow a maximum of $72,911.

If your child has any credit card debt outstanding, the bank usually figures she will pay about 4% of the outstanding balance each month. If she owes $3,000, for example, the bank will tack $120 onto the monthly debt service expense.

1. Bankers Don't Bite Your child should get her loan preapproved by her banker before she begins shopping for a house. If you have a good relationship with a loan officer, you might recommend to your child that she make an appointment to see him. You can point out that when she does find a house she likes, she will be more likely to have her offer accepted by the seller if she already has been preapproved by a bank.

She may be nervous about talking about her finances with him. Maybe she has made some mistakes with her money management that she is embarrassed about. Tell her not to worry. Not only have bankers seen all kinds of crazy loan applications, but they are in the business of lending money, and they have never been more creative and competitive in trying to write good loans than they have been in the last few years. Hopefully, he will be able to work with your child to get her the loan she needs. If not, at least he can point out why now might not be a good time for her to apply, and what she can do in the future to make her chance of being approved more likely.

2. Fifteen-Year Mortgage Once she has received preapproval from a lender, there is another thing you can do that will save her thousands of dollars, yet cost you absolutely nothing: suggest she try to qualify for a fifteen-year mortgage instead of one for thirty years. The advantages to this are:

- She will save thousands of dollars in interest
- She will build equity in her home at a faster rate
- The interest rate will probably be lower

Let's compare two mortgage scenarios. Say your daughter has $30,000 to put down on a $150,000 house. The interest rate on a $120,000 thirty-year fixed mortgage is 8%, and a fifteen-year is 7.5%. The monthly payment and interest paid will look like this:

	Monthly Payment	Interest Paid
15 years	$1,112	$ 80,160
30 years	−880	−196,800
Difference	$ 232	($116,640)

In addition you can point out what her house situation will look like if she sells her house in five years, after a 3% annual appreciation in the value of her home:

	15 years	30 years
Value of home	$173,891	$173,891
Selling commission (6%)	−10,433	−10,433
Net amount	$163,458	$163,458
Loan outstanding	−93,715	−114,083
Total net	$ 69,743	$ 49,375

She will have over $20,000 more to use to purchase a new home! If she plans on putting 20% down when she buys her next home, this extra money could buy an extra $100,000 in home value. If she chooses to stay in the same house for fifteen years, her fifteen-year mortgage will be paid in full. Yet the thirty-year will still have an outstanding balance of $92,137!

Despite the overwhelming evidence to the advantages of a fifteen-year mortgage, don't be surprised if your child still isn't too wild about the idea. Although the interest savings are dramatic, the higher monthly payment of a fifteen-year mortgage will affect the "28% and 36%" rules that bankers use to determine the maximum allowable loan. In the above example, that extra $232 per month for the fifteen-year mortgage (versus the thirty-year) reduces the maximum mortgage your child qualifies for by over $25,000. Only the wisest of young adults will be able to scale their target home price back by this large an amount.

3. Cosigning the Loan This sounds easy—no money out of your pocket, and your kid still gets to buy the house. But if your child needs your help to buy a house and you can't afford to give her any money, you (and she) may be better off waiting until she can afford the house on her own merit. The reason is that when you cosign a loan, you have just taken out the loan yourself, in the eyes of the law. If your child misses a payment (or defaults on the loan entirely), it goes on your credit report.

Other than taking over the payments yourself, there is no way to avoid this event. I have seen families forever divided over a parent's cosigning a loan for the child. The child falls on some financial hardship, the parent can't afford to make the payments, and the house is sold for less than the mortgage amount. I'm sure that many other first-time home buyers have had success using this method, but it should be considered only with a great deal of caution.

Thinking "Outside the Box"

There are also a couple of ways you can encourage your child to begin building home equity without buying a house, and without using your money.

1. Go Condo? Many first-time home buyers might be looking to purchase a condominium. These types of residences carry much less stigma than they did ten or twenty years ago. Nevertheless, if your child is considering buying a condo you should suggest she take the following steps:

- Have a trusted insurance agent review the certificate of insurance.
- Spend the $100 or so to have an attorney go over the bylaws and explain them to your child in plain English.

2. "I Don't Care How the Other Half Lives, as Long as They Pay My Mortgage" If your child is determined to begin building home equity but finds herself unable to afford a regular single-family home, you may wish to point out the wisdom of buying a duplex, living in one side and renting out the other. But before she does this she should seriously consider the positive and negative aspects of being a landlord.

Using Your Own Money to Help Your Child Buy a Home

Rarely does an adult child have all the money necessary to make a proper first-time home purchase. Usually the need or desire to own a home arises before she achieves the higher income, lower consumer debt level, and large down payment necessary to buy a home. In preparing to make that big purchase, most of us went through the anxiety of scrimping on things until we paid off our credit cards or other loans. Then we handed over our life savings in the form of the down payment.

A little struggle makes her appreciate the significance of the endeavor, but if you are reading this book you probably would like to augment your child's financial situation in any way you can. You can use hundreds, thousands, or hundreds of thousands of dollars, depending on your level of wealth and your desire to help your child.

1. Make a Mortgage Payment To get the biggest long-term bang for your buck (with no other commitment on your part), you may want to make an extra mortgage payment for your child. A $1,000 payment is certainly a generous gift, but the financial power behind this simple gesture may surprise you.

Go back to our example of your child's getting a $120,000 thirty-year mortgage at 8% fixed. The monthly payment would be about $880. When your child has moved into her new house, you could make a check out to her bank, and either give it to her or deliver it to the financial institution yourself (make sure she is aware of your generosity so her bookkeeping records don't get screwed up!).

Assuming your child continues to make her payments according to the established schedule, you have just taken ten months off her thirty-year mortgage and saved her $8,800 in payments. You can continue to do this at your convenience, but the earlier you do it, the greater long-term effect it has. There is no guarantee your child won't skip making a payment every time you do this, but the worst-case scenario is that you might buy her a few "free" months to tide her over during a short-term crunch.

2. Helping with the Down Payment This is one of the most common ways parents help their children buy homes. Many people in their twenties or thirties have the income needed to afford a home, and their credit is in decent enough shape. But because they are relatively recent entrants to the full-time workforce, their nest egg is probably not as big as they would like it to be.

A relaxed lending climate has meant that this does not preclude your child from getting a mortgage. Indeed, where bankers would once shy away from applicants with anything less than 15 or 20% of the purchase price, they now are sometimes lending with no down payment whatsoever.

That doesn't mean your child won't benefit if you boost the size of the down payment. First, unless your child is able to put at least 20% of the purchase price in the down payment, she will probably be required to purchase private mortgage insurance (PMI), which will guarantee the banker will get his money back if your child can't repay the loan. This might cost about $50 per month on a $120,000 loan, and is in effect until your child's equity in the home reaches 20%. If it takes a twenty-five-year-old four years to reach 20% equity, the PMI payments total $2,400. And they would be worth $90,763 when your child turns sixty-five, if the money had instead gone into a Roth IRA earning 10% annually.

Giving your child enough money to reach the 20% equity level can actually *lower* her monthly payment, and not just because the borrowed amount is less. Many lenders are happy to loan to an applicant with a down payment of only 5 or 10% of the purchase price. But because the bank is taking a higher risk in making this loan, it may charge a higher interest rate than it would if your child had the full 20%.

Helping with a down payment is also a good idea if it will prevent your child from withdrawing money from an IRA, or getting a loan from a 401(k). As shown in the examples in Chapter 8 and Chapter 9, a little money taken from those plans at an early age can have disastrous long-term ramifications on your child's retirement. Yet retirement is such a long way off and the house purchase is *right now*, so it is easy to understand why a first-time home buyer would consider this a viable option. Nevertheless, do whatever you can do to prevent her from taking this drastic step.

If you are loaning the money for the down payment, you should treat it as such, complete with documentation. Prepare a simple one-page agreement for your child to sign, stating the amount, payment period, and agreed-upon interest rate. The banker may want to know how your child was able to get this money, and may count the monthly payment for this loan against her maximum debt-service payment total. If the money is a gift, you should not give an amount over the annual $10,000 limit. But if you are married your spouse can also give $10,000. And if your child is married, you can also give $10,000 to her spouse. If you and your child are married, you can give your kid and her spouse up to $40,000 per year.

3. Shared Equity This is a relatively uncommon way for a parent to help a child purchase a house, but in the right situation it deserves a closer look. Basically, you and your child buy a house together. You each own half the house. Your child pays half the costs, plus rent (based on local market rates) for the other half. You get some of the great deductions that go along with owning rental property. And you can even "gift" the amount of the child's rent *back* to your kid, subject to the annual $10,000 limits.

There are a couple of "paperwork" steps you should take to protect you and your child from each other, and to make sure the transaction holds up to scrutiny from the folks at the IRS. You need to hire an attorney to draw up an agreement between you and your child. You will also need wills and living wills for both of you (see Chapter 3) so that in the event either of you dies, the next owners of your shares in the house are clearly defined. Unless you are well versed in landlord tax issues, you will need to enlist the services of a competent accountant to help you wade through the corresponding tax breaks.

Finally, if your kid cannot fulfill her obligations, you are the money source of last resort. The burden of the mortgage rests on your shoulders, and on your credit report.

4. First National Bank of Mom and Dad I have a client who lived in a small town. There was only one bank in the community, where the man had about $80,000 in certificates of deposit. The man's son was going to buy a house in the same community, and was approved for a mortgage at the same bank the client used. But before his son signed the mortgage agreement, the father called me up and said, "I have $80,000 in CDs at that bank earning 5%. My son is about to take out an $80,000 mortgage at 9%. Am I missing something, or is the bank making almost as much on my money as I am?"

I explained that the equation wasn't quite as simple as it seemed. The bank was a business and needed to make a profit. His son was not a no-risk borrower (no one is), and yet the client's CDs were very safe. And the father's CDs were short-term, while his son wanted a thirty-year mortgage. The father listened to me patiently, and then hung up the phone, called the bank, cashed out his CDs, and loaned the money to his son at 7.5%. That was a few years ago, and as far as I know everybody is happy with the arrangement (except the banker).

If you are in a position to make this same decision, it may be a good idea for you, too. You may earn a little more on your money, and at the same time save your child some interest expense. In addition, your child won't have to deal with the loan application process; won't pay "points," fees, and other closing costs; and won't miss out on owning her ideal home, just because she didn't yet have preapproved borrower status.

Do you want to loan money to your child, but you're not sure she's a good credit risk? Have her apply for preapproval at a bank, even if you plan to lend her the money. If she gets a thumbs-up, you should be okay. But if the bank turns her down, you might want to rethink why *you* would be so excited to lend her the money.

Before you make this loan, you should make sure you stay on the good side of the IRS (that seems like good advice, no matter what). Uncle Sam's curiosity is piqued whenever you are making intergenerational transfers of money, even if it is just a loan.

The tax laws say that you can charge whatever interest rate you want, or even not charge anything at all. But the IRS has an interest rate that they want you to charge. It is reset monthly, and you can find out the "applicable federal interest rates" at www.irs.gov. Basically, you can figure on its being within a quarter of a percent of whatever the thirty-year Treasury bond is paying (there are other rates for shorter-term loans). You can avoid a lot of headaches by charging the rate prescribed by the IRS.

If you choose to charge anything less than the minimum prescribed amount, in the eyes of the IRS you are giving money to your child. The amount of the "gift" is the difference between what you are charging and what the IRS states the applicable federal rate is. If the loan is under $10,000, you don't have to worry about the applicable federal rate (as long as the total of all loans to your child are less than $10,000).

If the loan is more than $10,000 but less than $100,000, you can use a different rule. Basically, if your child's annual net investment income is less than $1,000, then the required interest amount is zero. If it is more than $1,000 then the required interest amount is equal to whatever your child's net investment income was. Be careful with this—if your child has a $20,000 bank account earning 5%, she'll exceed the $1,000 limit. It is best to have an accountant look over your child's tax returns (or even prepare them, paid for by your child) to make sure that all interest income is accounted for.

If the loan is more than $100,000, you are stuck using the applicable federal rate as the benchmark. Regardless of the interest rate you set, watch how far you stray from the one set by the IRS. The difference between the IRS rate and yours is counted as income to your child, and is taxed accordingly. In addition, it counts toward the $10,000 annual gift limit. It seems that simply charging the applicable federal rate is pretty fair to you and your child, and avoids a lot of scrutiny from the IRS.

After you've taken steps to placate the good people at the Internal Revenue Service, you should then take a preemptive strike at avoiding any conflict with your child. The issues with your child will arise when she is late on a payment (assume this is going to happen, and then you can be pleasantly surprised if it doesn't). You will be hard-pressed to avoid second-guessing your child's money sense, and will start taking an interest in where her money is actually going, when it should be going to you first and foremost. Too many incidents like this, and you find yourselves returning to a parent/child relationship that you both want to avoid.

Once you reconcile these issues and reach an interest rate that is acceptable to you, your child, and the IRS, there are a few more cautionary measures:

• Document the loan. This must include a promissory note signed by both of you, stating the amount, interest rate, and length of the loan.

• Secure the loan. A lawyer can help you do this, but basically you state that your child's ownership of the qualified home is security for the debt, and that the home will satisfy the debt if your child defaults on the payments. Your child needs this step if she wants to deduct the interest on the mortgage for her tax purposes.

• Designate the loan as a "demand" loan (this means you reserve the right to ask for full payment of the outstanding balance at any time, rather than only on a certain date). If you miss this step the IRS can add up the interest over the stated life of the loan and count it as a gift in one year.

• Write a note to yourself saying that your child was solvent at the time you made the loan. This demonstrates that this wasn't a gift, it was a loan, and by God, you fully expected to be paid.

All of this might seem like unnecessary headaches and paperwork, but you are taking these steps to protect yourself and your child in the event something goes wrong.

And heaven help you if something does prevent your child from paying you according to the terms of the loan. If your child does get into a financial bind and can't pay you on time, you should talk with her and offer to help her sort out her mess. But by no means should you just stop collecting the loan and forget about it. The unpaid balance will become a gift in the eyes of the IRS, and you or your child will be liable for the corresponding gift taxes. Of course, at least you get to firmly demand that the loan be paid back, while blaming the evil IRS!

If your child gets into a hole and there is no other solution to your child's predicament, she will need to sell the house. Hopefully the net proceeds will be enough to pay off your loan, and the two of you can walk away from the matter a little wiser. Regardless of what action you think you are going to take, if your child's financial situation begins to look shaky you should contact your lawyer to protect not only your interests but hers as well.

How Do You Save Today to Help Buy a House Tomorrow?

If you want to practice some "mental accounting" and set up an account to help your child's future home purchase, you can use just about any investment method, starting with a mutual fund (Chapter 1). But if you are going to be over 59½ by the time your child buys a house, a variable annuity (Chapter 4) in your own name or your own Roth IRA (Chapter 5) gives you a way to keep control of the money, but delays or avoids any taxation on the earnings.

Getting Started

If your child is nearing a time where it is appropriate to think about buying her first home, this may be the first moment in her adult life where she admits that you might actually know something she doesn't. If you handle the situation right, your love and wisdom can save her a lot of anguish and money. You can take satisfaction in helping her make the biggest purchase of her life. Go gently, and if you think you might offend her (or her spouse), keep your mouth shut (this home might be where you are cared for in your declining years!).

chapter eleven

Dying to Make Your Kid a Millionaire

Tools the Wealthy Use to Cut Estate Taxes

Imagine yourself in your golden years. Looking back on your life, you have something to be proud of. You worked hard, saved money, and invested wisely. You don't feel "rich" but you might describe yourself as "comfortable." You were hesitant to give your kids any significant amounts of money before, but now you've realized that your wealth is growing quickly and you've got more than enough to live your life under your terms.

Your children have matured into wise and responsible adults, and you are pleased at the sizable portfolio you will be passing to them. You envision the kids sitting in your attorney's office after you're gone, remembering you fondly as the lawyer reads the details of your considerable estate.

Unfortunately, if you pass away without making plans, Uncle Sam will be at that meeting, too, and he will be listening just as intently as your children, looking for his share. And the government could get a bigger portion of your assets than any of your kids do.

• • •

When George W. Bush, Jr., arrived in the White House, the debate over estate taxes reached new levels. Critics cried that estate taxes were unfair, wreaking the most havoc on family farms and small businesses, and causing citizens to waste time and money on legal fees and insurance. They argued that the government was destroying the "American Dream" of building a better life for our future generations.

Proponents of the tax, though, pointed out how few estates actually paid taxes, and the estates that did were usually only those of the *very* rich. Advocates of estate taxes said most Americans weren't concerned that the children of Bill Gates might inherit "only" a billion dollars, and that untaxed, huge amounts of transferred wealth would only serve to spoil the second and third generations.

In 2001 legislation was passed that raised the ceiling of assets exempt from estate taxes, reduced the top rate, and eliminated the federal tax altogether in 2010. But unless the law is extended, the legislation requires estate taxes to be *reinstated* in 2011.

Will Your Family Be Affected?

Regardless of your view on the issue, you may not have paid much attention to how estate taxes might reduce the money you leave to your children. You may have looked at the laws, listened to the political rhetoric, and decided that this is one tax that won't concern you. There might be some logic to your decision—according to the IRS, there were 2,300,000 deaths in 1997, and only about 43,000 cases (2%) of those estates paid any estate taxes.

Part of your overlooking estate taxes may stem from your confidence that the government will follow through with plans to repeal or at least greatly reduce the tax.

But estate taxes won't just be erased from the tax code with no ramifications. They've been around in some form for over two hundred years—according to *The Wall Street Journal,* Americans first started paying "death taxes" in 1797. And the modern estate tax has been around since 1916, when it was implemented to help pay for World War I.

Even if the estate tax is repealed or reduced, under current law there will be a long phase-out period. During that phase-out period, there is certainly a chance that the changing political and economic landscape would cause *reinstatement* of taxes on estates. Unless you can guarantee that you or your spouse won't die before the phase-out of the estate tax is complete, you need to consider the tax part of reality.

You may also have disregarded estate taxes because of the unified credit, which allows part of your assets to escape the tax (in 2002, any estates under $1,000,000 will pass to the designated heirs exempt from the tax). You may be aware of this figure and decide that your estate will never get that big, so you won't have to be concerned.

But assuming an annual gain of 6% in their net worth, a fifty-year-old couple with an $800,000 net worth today could see their estate top $2 million in fifteen years. At a 15% annual increase, a thirty-five-year-old couple with a $100,000 net worth today would have a portfolio of over $13 million by the time the couple reaches seventy.

Even if your net worth is much less than the exempted amount, estate taxes may still concern you. Why? Because if you follow my rule of thumb (described in Chapter 3) for the amount of money you need to leave to a minor child, your estate will be well into seven figures for *each* child you have. If you or your spouse are the owners of the life insurance and you both die, up to half of the policy proceeds could go to your state and federal government!

Finally, you may feel that although your estate would be vulnerable to taxation at your death, it doesn't bother you. You're okay with your heirs' sending a chunk of their inheritance to the federal government. That's your prerogative, of course, but deciding to do nothing is still a decision.

A prudent move, though, is to play it safe and assume that some form of estate tax will be around when you die.

What Can You Do?

The reason only about 2% of estates pay taxes each year is not because only 2% of people have a net worth over the exempt amount. Many people have assets worth much more than several hundred thousand dollars.

It's because people's attitudes about estate taxes are the same as their feelings about any other tax: They don't want to pay any more than they have to.

Think about it. In any year, on April 15, at 11:30 P.M., as you are driving to the post office to get your return in on time, have you ever said to yourself, "Boy, it sure was a great year to be an American. I think I'll write a check for a few thousand more than what I already owe, just to show my appreciation. Kind of a big ol' tip for Uncle Sam!" I think this would be an ideal way to qualify for an IRS audit.

It sounds crazy, but that is no different from avoiding the opportunity to reduce taxes on your estate, especially when the tactics are relatively simple and cost-effective (and definitely so when weighed against the hundreds of thousands of dollars of estate taxes your children might pay).

The most popular ways to reduce the blow of estate taxes to your family's financial security are:

- Maximizing the unified credit
- Giving the money to your heirs during your life
- Establishing a qualified personal residence trust (QPRT)
- Using life insurance proceeds

There is enough information here to get you a long way toward reducing or eliminating estate taxes. Eventually, though, you should plan on spending at least an hour or two with a qualified estate-planning attorney to ensure that your moves are as effective as possible, and legally airtight.

The Marriage Loophole

Estate taxes don't kick in until you die. And even when you do pass away, you can transfer an unlimited amount of money to your spouse with no estate tax whatsoever. Don't take this to mean Uncle Sam has gone soft on surviving husbands and wives. The federal government allows this because they know that, if a family does nothing, there will be a big check sent to Washington when the second spouse dies.

For many good but uninformed families, the scenario looks like this: the first spouse to die (usually the husband) leaves everything to the wife. When she dies, the government collects taxes on her estate. Her heirs get a little break, as the government does let certain amounts of money pass tax-free to beneficiaries (again, in 2002 the "exempt amount"—the value of an estate any one person can leave to heirs with no estate taxation—is $1,000,000).

But anywhere from one third to one half of assets over that amount can go to the federal government in the form of estate taxes. And regardless of reduction or repeal, your state may impose its own tax in additional to the federal one, making the hit even worse.

Families in the know realize the exempt amount is a valuable tool because it applies to each *person*, not each couple. Let's say a couple has a $2,000,000 net worth, when they die in 2002 or 2003. They can each leave $1,000,000 to their kids, tax-free. When compared to leaving all the assets to the surviving spouse, the difference in tax dollars paid under this scenario is amazing:

Scenario 1 All assets left to surviving spouse	$2,000,000
Approximate federal estate tax when	
surviving spouse dies:	–435,000
Net to heirs	$1,565,000

Scenario 2 $1,000,000 left to spouse,	
$1,000,000 to heirs	$2,000,000
Approximate federal estate tax when	
surviving spouse dies:	–0
Net to heirs	$2,000,000

Over four hundred thousand dollars more for their children in the second scenario, and it is perfectly legal! But you must take special steps to maximize the benefits of this kind of maneuver for your heirs.

First, you should retitle some of your assets, especially if, like many couples, you and your spouse have all your money and possessions jointly held. Joint ownership is great for the marriage but lousy for avoiding estate taxes. You should split the assets so that each of you owns a fairly equal amount, when measured in dollar values.

Once you have split the assets, your next step is to establish what is known as a "family bypass trust" with your heirs as the beneficiaries. In other words, you should add a provision to your will stating that when the first spouse dies (no matter if it's the husband or wife), an amount equal to the current exempt amount (like $1,000,000 in 2002) will bypass the surviving spouse and go directly to the family bypass trust. The remainder of the assets will remain with the surviving spouse.

Be careful when stating in your will that the bypass trust should receive the "current exempt amount." Because this amount will go up and down depending on the tax laws, you may end up unintentionally leaving all of your money to your children, with nothing for your spouse. It is better to update your will annually, using the exact dollar amount that equals the current exemption.

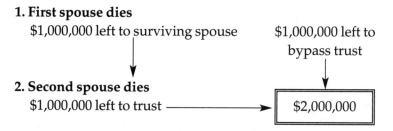

A couple with $2,000,000 net worth

1. First spouse dies
$1,000,000 left to surviving spouse $1,000,000 left to bypass trust

2. Second spouse dies
$1,000,000 left to trust ⟶ $2,000,000

3. Trust assets are then distributed to heirs

What happens if the widow (or widower) needs the money from the bypass trust? You can add language to the trust to give the surviving spouse three ways to get access without losing exemption from estate taxation:

- **All income**   This gives her the right to take any dividends and interest generated by the trust assets.
- **The right to annually withdraw** the greater of $5,000 or 5% of trust assets
- **The "MESH" opportunity**   She can withdraw whatever amount necessary for her maintenance, education, support, and health care.

Although the surviving spouse can legally get at the money in the trust for the above reasons, she should first use her own assets for her living expenses. The money in the family bypass trust has already escaped estate taxes, but any assets in her name greater than the exempt amount at her death will be subject to estate taxation.

Give It Away

When I discuss estate planning with my clients, some people say, "I'm not worried about estate taxes. When I get sick, I'll just sign all my money over to my kids, and by the time I die I'll be broke. No money, no taxes."

A nice idea, but the IRS has already made sure that giving money away on your deathbed will not allow you to avoid taxation.

The government quashes this end-around through the use of the "gift tax." The gift tax is combined with the estate tax to ensure that you and your heirs pay an identical amount of taxes on the transfer of assets, regardless of whether you give the money during your life or at your death. That doesn't mean you can't give any money away without being taxed on it—you get the exemption amount as the estate tax exemption (for instance, $1,000,000 in 2002). But you and your spouse can each give only that total exempted amount during your lives and at death, before the gift/estate tax will hit your family.

That doesn't mean every penny of gifted money is subject to the gift tax. There is a nice feature in the tax code called "the annual exclusion," which allows a person to give anyone else up to $10,000 per year with no effect on the exempt amount. Married people can each give up to $10,000 to as many people as they like, so you and your spouse can give your child (or anybody else) $20,000 per year before you are affected by the gift tax.

This annual exclusion can be a potent estate planning tool, and the sooner you give the money away, the more powerful the effect. Because when you give money to someone else, you are not only reducing your estate (and thus the taxes on it) by the gifted amount, but you are also giving the total of earnings the money would have generated over your lifetime. A $10,000 gift given twenty years ago, earning 10% annually, is worth over $67,000 today. And no gift or estate taxes would ever be paid by the recipient on that amount.

The best types of assets to be given are ones that you expect to grow dramatically in value over time. A good place to start might be shares of common stock in a growth company, or shares of a growth-oriented mutual fund. However, if you have investments with a low cost basis, you may want to avoid giving them away while you're alive, because the recipient also gets your original purchase price as their new cost basis. It is better to transfer highly appreciated assets *after* you die, because the recipient's new cost basis will be the value on the date of your death, and that will probably be much higher than what you originally paid.

In 2002, under the 2001 tax law changes, up to $3 million of assets left to a surviving spouse and $1.3 million left to other beneficiaries receive a stepped-up cost basis at the donor's death. But for amounts over that limit, the heir gets the donor's basis and will owe capital gains tax when the asset is sold.

Giving assets to your child might make sense, but you may be concerned with what your kid does with the money, especially if he is a minor. After all, under the law, you have no say in what your child does with the money and you can't take it back. But the legal experts already have a solution for your dilemma: Don't give the money directly to your child. Instead, place the assets in a trust with the child as the beneficiary. The different types of protective trusts are covered in Chapter 12.

Keeping a Home in the Family

Some of my clients want to make sure their adult children inherit a family home or vacation property but are concerned about the amount of estate taxes their heirs will pay on the residence. There are a few ways that you can get the property out of your estate and into the hands of your children, while still avoiding any taxation. Proper execution of these strategies allows you not only to ensure that a home stays in your family but also to:

- Remove the asset from your estate, along with any future appreciation in value
- Avoid the gift tax

1. Buying on Installment You can transfer your real estate to your kid by financing an installment sale, where your child pays you monthly or annually for the value of the purchase. The IRS requires that the sale price be for fair market value; otherwise, the difference between the market price and the actual sales price (for a few hundred dollars, a real estate property appraiser will work with you to establish what the "market" price of the home is) will be considered a gift.

If you qualify for the exclusion of long-term gains on a personal residence, you can shelter up to $250,000 (or $500,000 if you're married). You must also charge your child a minimum interest rate (available at www.irs.gov) on the outstanding balance of the loan, although the required rate is usually substantially lower than prevailing rates from financial institutions (see also Chapter 10).

Your child doesn't have enough money to afford the installment payments? No problem. You can use the annual exclusion to give up to $10,000 to each child each year, and your spouse can do the same. And if you choose to remain in the property, you must pay your child market-rate rent to stay. This money can help your child make the payments. But you and your child must create a paper trail, complete with separate checks for the note payments made to you, and any gifts or rent payments you make to your kid. This documentation will provide proof to the IRS that you and your child have a legitimate business transaction.

2. The QPRT A "cleaner" way to get your house out of your estate and into the hands of your child while continuing to live there is through a qualified personal residence trust (QPRT). This more-complex tool allows you to place your primary residence (or even a cottage or second home) into a trust with your child as the beneficiary. You retain the right to live in the house, rent-free, for several years, after which you will have to pay rent. The value of the house (less the value of the rent-free living) given to your child can trigger a gift tax, but you can also use part of your $10,000 exemption to avoid the gift tax.

There are a few other negative aspects to this method. Placing your home in a QPRT removes your opportunity to sell the home and take the lifetime capital gains exclusion (up to $500,000 for married couples). And because the house was given (rather than sold) to the trust, your child inherits your original cost basis (what you first paid for the house). If you were to die with your house in your name without using the QPRT, your child's cost basis in the house would be the value on the date of your death—a higher cost basis means fewer capital gains, and fewer capital gains taxes. Finally, you must outlive the length of the trust; otherwise, the house remains part of your estate.

Most important, you must give up control over an asset to get it out of your estate. You certainly must trust your child to give him ownership of money or stocks, but be extra careful when relinquishing ownership of your house. Theoretically, when your child is the owner, he can kick you out whenever he feels like it.

Life Insurance

Although you bought that whole-life policy years ago, it seems like only yesterday that the insurance agent sat with you at your kitchen table while your kids peeked at him from the hallway. He pretended not to mind when your dog kept jumping up on his lap. He told you what a nice house you had, accepted your offer of a cup of coffee, and eventually got around to the subject of insurance. He talked about how safe his company was, how competitive the rates were, and how concerned he was about what would become of your family if anything were to happen to you or your spouse. Maybe you agreed with him, or maybe you were just tired and wanted to go to bed, but you signed the papers and began making the premium payments.

Now the kids are grown, you've moved three times, and the dog is dead. You might be thinking about discontinuing those payments for these reasons:

- Your policy generates enough annual dividends to cover the premiums
- You decided to reduce the death benefit
- Your insurance needs aren't as large as in the past

Don't give up just yet.

If you want to make your child wealthy at your death, you could be sitting on a gold mine. And if you want to save hundreds of thousands of dollars of estate taxes, you may even want to purchase more life insurance.

What to Do with the Insurance You Have

First, examine your current policy. As I pointed out in Chapter 3, cash-value life insurance is extremely expensive for younger people, especially when compared with term rates. Don't feel bad if you bought a cash-value policy way back when—term may have hardly existed when you bought your policy, and expensive insurance was better than none at all.

As you enter the autumn of your life, you are starting to get a good deal on that cash-value policy. Even the skeptical experts at the Consumer Federation of America admit that after twenty years of premium payments, cash-value life insurance (like whole life) starts to work in your favor. If you don't think so, call an agent up and tell him you want to purchase a new whole-life policy identical to the one you already have. Because of your age, the rates he quotes you will probably be many times what you are already paying on your current policy.

The good news about using a cash-value policy to enrich your child is that you have never paid income taxes on the accumulating money inside the policy. And when you die your child, as the beneficiary, will receive the proceeds of the policy tax-free. That's the good news.

The bad news is if the ownership of the insurance is set up like most policies, your child will not be able to avoid estate taxes on the proceeds.

Here's why: the IRS checks your "incidents of ownership" (your ties to the life insurance) to decide if you have an interest in the policy. If you are the owner of the policy or you pay the premiums, it becomes part of your taxable estate. You can make your spouse the owner, but if your kid is the beneficiary, upon your death the IRS will say your spouse has made a "gift" of the insurance proceeds to your child, and your family will be liable for a hefty tax. Your only allowable part in this process is to serve as the insured (and eventually die).

So what can you do with your current insurance? You must get it out of your estate. If you or your spouse is the owner of the policy, it will be included in one of your estates. So you obviously want to make your child the owner of the policy. But that act has a couple drawbacks:

1. A Potential Gift Tax Making your child the owner results in a taxable gift to your kid in the amount of the current cash value of the policy (the amount is on your most recent statement). In the best case you will unnecessarily use up part of your unified credit. In the worst case, you may have to pay a gift tax.

2. Loss of Ownership You don't have any say in what happens to the policy. Your kid can cash in the insurance and do whatever he pleases with the money.

You can avoid the gift tax issue by having your child buy the policy from you for the cash value. But the drawback of this is that when you die, your child will have to pay income tax on the proceeds of the life insurance.

ILIT A better solution is to create an Irrevocable Life Insurance Trust (ILIT). You draw up the trust papers with an attorney, and name a trustee (not you or your spouse). This doesn't help you avoid a possible gift tax on the cash value of the policy, but at least you get a chance to dictate exactly what can and can't be done with the policy and its proceeds. Keep in mind, though, that the terms you decide can't ever be changed, and you can never regain ownership of the policy.

That's why they call it "irrevocable."

Regardless of whether you give your policy to your child or to an ILIT, do yourself and your family a big favor and try not to die for three years after the transfer. If you do, the insurance policy goes back into your estate. Then again, that may not be your biggest concern at the time.

New Insurance Assuming you are still insurable, it might be better to remain the owner of your current policy, and plan on keeping it in your estate. Instead, create an ILIT and have the trustee purchase a new policy on your life. Wealthy people with the following issues often use this method:

• *Illiquid assets* A family with a farm or business that makes up a large portion of their net worth may not be able to avoid estate taxes. Yet the family also doesn't want to sell their business just to raise funds to pay the tax. So they have the trustee of an ILIT buy an insurance policy in the trust on the business owner's life with a death benefit equal to what the estate tax bill would be. When the owner dies the beneficiaries of the trust cash in the insurance, pay the government, and still keep the farm or business in the family.

• *Big IRA* Even if the estate tax is repealed or a family's assets are below the exempt amount, heirs will owe income taxes on withdrawals from inherited IRAs or 401(k)s. Some people will choose to buy life insurance in the amount equal to what the tax bill would be.

• *Investment considerations*   The family may currently have enough cash to pay any estate taxes, but they might decide it is a better bet to pay a few thousand dollars in insurance premiums each year and keep the rest of the liquid cash available for other future needs.

There is another potential benefit to creating an ILIT to own life insurance. You can use cash or the sales proceeds from some other asset you have (like stocks or mutual funds) as the source for the premium payments. Every dollar spent on premiums is one less dollar to be grabbed by the government.

The payment of the premiums for insurance owned by a trust is a potentially sticky matter. If you or your spouse pays the premium directly to the insurance company, your actions may be determined to be incidents of ownership by the IRS, and the policy proceeds will be taxed as part of your estate.

If you wish to avoid the issue of setting up a trust, you may want to follow the example of a businessman I worked with. He and I held a meeting with his adult children, their spouses, his attorney, and his insurance agent. We explained to the kids the terms of the man's will, what they might inherit when the man died, and the effect estate taxes would have on their inheritances. Then we told them how we could use life insurance to offset the damage the government would do to their potential wealth. The man told his family if they wanted to save a substantial amount of money, they might want to pay for insurance on his life (we also pointed out that if anything suspicious happened to my client, the kids better have airtight alibis).

The children agreed to the proposition and began paying the premiums. If your children have some extra cash, you may want them to demonstrate their financial wisdom. Perhaps they will realize that few thousand dollars a year could save them hundreds of thousands of dollars in estate taxes, and they will find a way to come up with the money.

If your children can't or won't pay for the insurance, that doesn't necessarily preclude you from helping the kids pay the premiums. You (and your spouse) can use your $10,000 annual gift exclusion to make up the difference between what your children can afford to pay and the annual premium payment. And if you choose to use an ILIT, you can make annual gifts to the trust of up to $5,000 per beneficiary, and the trustee can make the premium payments from those gifts (subject to the rules of a Crummey Trust—see Chapter 12).

For example: If your daughter, her husband, and their two children are the beneficiaries, you can give up to $40,000 per year to them, and your spouse can do the same. Be careful, though, to make no legal direction as to how the money is spent. If the IRS can show that you ordered the money to be used for insurance premiums only, the policy may be included in your estate. Try to use gentle encouragement and education with your children. If they still don't pay the premiums and let the policy lapse, they can suffer the consequences.

Cash Value or Term? As is the case whenever you purchase life insurance, when using an ILIT you still have to choose between cash-value life insurance and term. A term policy can still be pretty tempting: a sixty-year-old man in good health can pick up a million dollars of twenty-year term for as little as $6,000 per year in premiums. A fit woman of the same age would be able to get the same deal for less than $4,000 per year.

But increasing your "after-estate-tax" bequest is usually best served by cash-value life insurance, such as whole life or universal life. If you buy twenty-year term at age sixty and die before you reach eighty, the beneficiaries of your ILIT get $1 million with no income taxes, no estate taxes, and no problems (other than the loss of your company).

But if you put term insurance in the ILIT, and then make things difficult by dying *after* you turn eighty, your family will get nothing and your premium payments will have been wasted. You can try to take out a new term policy when the first one expires, but the premiums will be so high and the health restrictions so tight that you might as well just skip the insurance company and give the premium payments directly to your heirs.

The cash-value policy is the better choice for use in an ILIT because it stays in effect as long as the premiums are paid. Once the insurance company agrees to underwrite your life with a fixed-premium policy, it can't raise your premiums beyond the amount stated in the contract. And if the insurance company earns more than it expects on your payments, you may be able to stop paying the premiums altogether (but don't count on it).

If your death today might incur estate taxes, yet you feel that the tax may be repealed, you may want to buy "convertible term" life insurance within the ILIT. This type of policy is much cheaper than traditional cash-value life insurance, yet you still have an option to convert the policy to cash value if repeal of the estate tax doesn't hold.

College Factor

In Chapter 2 you can read about a great opportunity to get money (and the future earnings) out of your estate, keep control of the money, avoid any gift taxes, and help your child pay for college by using the Section 529 or Qualified State Tuition Plans.

Getting Started

Estate planning is an important part of the financial process, but it is crucial if you think your heirs will be subject to estate taxes. Future legislation may assist you in passing your assets to your family tax-free, but don't forget that what the government gives, it can also take away with a change in the political climate.

You will need to consult with an attorney to know how the current laws may affect you and your family. Not just any lawyer will do—choose one who not only specializes in estate planning but also is familiar with the laws of the state in which you reside.

You should also review and update your estate plan in the following circumstances:

- You move to a new state
- Your intentions for your heirs change
- There is a significant change in estate tax law
- The "exempt amount" changes

Even if none of these events occurs, you should still plan to spend an hour or two with your estate-planning attorney every five years or so, just for an update.

Once your attorney has established your estate plan and potential estate tax liability, you should find an insurance agent to help you determine if he can help you accomplish your goals. Again, you need to find someone who is experienced in these matters. A Certified Financial Planner (CFP) or Chartered Life Underwriter (CLU) designation doesn't guarantee the individual is an expert at estate planning issues, but he will probably have more training in the complexities of tax law than the average agent.

PART FIVE
Extra Stuff

chapter twelve

Protecting Your Child's Wealth from Your Child

Give Your Kid the Right Amount of Money at the Right Time

The hope parents hold in their hearts when it comes to investing is palpable. When I first discuss saving for their children, talk always turns to building a portfolio that grows simultaneously with the development of their child's value system. Parents share dreams of their kid maturing into a responsible saver and prudent investor, tapping into the money only for the most sensible of objectives. The child may even expand the portfolio to unimagined heights, and eventually pass both substantial assets and financial wisdom to the next generation.

You probably have the same vision. A hundred years from now your portrait will hang above the nuclear reactor in the living room, and when visitors ask who's in the picture, your great-great-grandchild will say, "She built our fortune, starting with just a few lousy bucks in a mutual fund."

But along with all those warm and fuzzy dreams, you might also share a dark fear that some benevolent mothers and fathers have. As much as these parents love their kids, they worry that when their kids reach "adulthood," any amount of money in the hands of the children will be frittered away on dangerous cars, stupid friends, and spring breaks that last all year. Even if the assets survive a period of youthful indiscretion, parents see sons- and daughters-in-law as a threat to the children's financial future, through both marriage and divorce.

Most important, good and loving parents don't want to create lazy, spoiled children who have no motivation to get out of bed in the morning.

You obviously don't want to pamper your kid in a life of luxury. But then you are confronted with another dilemma in choosing how quickly you should transfer wealth to your child. If you keep all of your money in your control until you die, not only will you probably pay a higher rate of taxes on the year-to-year earnings than if the money were in your child's name, but at your death your family's assets will be more likely to be decimated by estate taxes.

You hope that through your superb parenting skills and your child's boundless intellect, your child's future will match your ideal scenario. And indeed, it is very important that you lead by example, and take the time to teach your child the best way to get rich and stay rich (see the Introduction and "Ten Things You Need to Know").

But you shouldn't rest your hopes solely on demonstration and education, any more than you would ask your three-year-old to carefully watch you chop vegetables, and then pass her the butcher knife.

Instead, employ the "trust, but verify" philosophy when giving your child gradual control over the money. There are three distinct phases to your child's life where you should decide if you are going to free up any of your assets to your child's supervision:

1. When she reaches adulthood
2. Sometime during her adulthood
3. At your death

Mark McGwire is one of the greatest home-run hitters in baseball history. But I'm willing to bet that when he was a toddler, his mom or dad didn't take him out to a baseball diamond, put him up at the plate, and have some pitcher blaze ninety-mile-an-hour fastballs under Mark's chin until he learned to belt it back out of the park. That might have garnered them a visit from the child protection authorities.

Instead, his parents probably did what most moms and dads do when they teach their little kids to hit. They started out a few feet away, gently lobbing a plastic ball right in the kid's strike zone. Sooner or later, he connected, drilling it back toward the parent. Wisely, mom or dad moved back a few more feet, throwing a little harder this time. Over the next several years, Mark moved from T-ball, to Little League, to high school baseball, and finally, to the major leagues. At each stage there were new challenges, but he could draw from what he learned at the previous level to meet those challenges and move on to greater heights.

Letting your child have a small amount of money in her late teens allows her to show you what she has learned, and minimizes the damage of any mistakes. As she grows older and more sensible, you can give her greater access to the money, coaching and guiding her along the way.

Besides, by using a philosophy of gradual release, you are giving your child money when it's meaningful. Making your kid a millionaire when she turns eighty-five isn't going to do nearly as much for her as $10,000 might on her twenty-first birthday.

Eventually, the inevitable will happen, and you will be dead. Hopefully, she will have become the responsible, intelligent person you wanted her to be and she will inherit the remainder of your estate. If not, you can pull a "Joan Crawford" and leave her the princely sum of $1 in your will (you should pursue this action only if you aren't afraid of her writing a "tell-all" biography about you).

• • •

You can't make your child a millionaire without eventually giving her the money. Whether used separately or together, the following methods of ownership will allow you to give your child meaningful amounts of money at appropriate times in her life, without risking harm to her future.

The UTMA/UGMA Account

This is the most common form of ownership for minor children. Technically, a minor cannot own money, assets, or property outright. In 1956 the Uniform Gifts to Minors Act (UGMA) created a simplified "trust" that allowed assets to be held in the name of a child, on the condition the child gains control of the assets upon reaching adulthood. The key word here is "uniform," as in the same for all states. The states resented any federal intrusion into their respective way of doing business, and began tinkering with the law.

In 1984 Congress passed the Uniform Transfers to Minors Act (UTMA) to correct some flaws in the UGMA. They recommended that states adopt the UTMA in place of the UGMA, and many complied. But some of the states modified the UTMA, and others stuck with the UGMA. What we are left with is a hodgepodge of laws and regulations, and which ones apply to your child depends on where your child lives when the account is established.

Regardless of your state's laws, one thing remains constant: placing money in an UTMA/UGMA account for your child is a completed gift. Although you act as the custodian, when your child reaches the age of termination, she can do whatever she pleases with the money. In legal terms the account dissolves when the child reaches eighteen or twenty-one, depending on the state of jurisdiction. Alaska, for one, allows you to specify an age from eighteen to twenty-five. Maybe not enough of a reason to pack your family up and move to Juneau, but you should check your state's laws to find out the applicable age of majority.

Some parents mistakenly believe they can make deposits into an UTMA/UGMA account when their children are small, and if the kids turn into moody, irresponsible, self-centered teenagers (it's been known to happen), the parents can just take the money back out of the account before the children reach adulthood. It is possible to do this, but you might just be better off calling the IRS and asking when you can stop by for an audit. It's the kids' money, and any attempt to retrieve control over it could mean extra taxes and penalties from the government.

Why, then, would anyone use this type of account? If you trust that your child will manage the money responsibly upon reaching adulthood, an UTMA/UGMA can be an excellent way to lower your family's tax bill. In an UTMA/UGMA account your child can earn up to $750 of interest, dividends, and capital gains each year tax-free. The next $750 are taxed at her rate, which is probably going to be the lowest bracket (15%). Any annual earnings over $1,500 (this number is raised for inflation, in $100 increments) are taxed at your highest bracket. Better yet, when your child turns fourteen, all of the earnings are taxed at her rate, which is still likely to be the lowest bracket.

A typical family's actual savings can be dramatic, especially if that family is in the upper tax brackets. Say a couple in the 27% income tax bracket and 20% capital gains tax bracket has a baby. They put $1,000 at her birth into a hypothetical mutual fund earning 10% per year, and the fund pays out 5% in income and short-term gains, and 5% in long-term gains at the end of each year. The couple will pay the taxes with funds outside of the account.

They continue to add $1,000 on her birthday each year, stopping with her seventeenth birthday. After eighteen years, this is how using the UTMA/UGMA account would save the family taxes, versus keeping the account in their own name:

	Parents' Name	**UTMA/UGMA**
Final amount	$49,059	$49,059
Total fed taxes paid	– 7,243	– 2,963
Net amount	$41,816	$46,096

This couple would save over $4,000 in taxes by putting the money in their child's name. And the amount would be almost $5,500 if they were in the 35% bracket.

After seeing this example, a parent might get giddy with delight at the idea of saving thousands of dollars in taxes while still keeping the money "in the family." Yet another may recoil in horror at the thought of irrevocably placing this much money in the hands of a young adult, just to save a few thousand dollars in taxes. They're both right.

Another reason to deposit the money in your child's name in an UTMA account is what I call the "attention factor." When I was fourteen I became interested in the stock market. My father never dabbled in investments, but he set up an account in his name with a few thousand dollars, and bought some stocks on my recommendations. It was a good learning experience for me, as I could begin following the stock in the paper and reading the company's annual reports. And I appreciated my dad's willingness to put up his hard-earned money to further my knowledge. I'm also happy that, after just a few decades, he has stopped bringing up the investment losses I incurred for him.

But it wasn't until I turned fifteen, when I had some money of my own, that my fascination with investing soared. I was making $5 an hour at the time, working in a furniture store, and I quickly realized that a $100 gain or loss was equal to about a week's pay. I knew I needed to learn as much as I could about the stock market. I enrolled in a night class on investing at a local community college, and began working after school at a brokerage firm (the same one that I work at today). I even started an investment club with some of my high school friends.

Your child may not have the same level of initial enthusiasm, but she will be much more interested in tracking an account that is in her name, and under her Social Security number. She will receive all of the statements and literature, and can access her account online. But make sure that until she is eighteen (or twenty-one, depending on your state), she checks all of her financial moves with you first.

College Factor

This is where money held in your child's name can actually be a liability. When your child goes to college, if you and she want to get any grants, loans, or scholarships, you will be required to fill out a form listing all the assets you own, as well as those owned in your child's UTMA/UGMA accounts (but not her IRAs, Roth IRAs, or annuities). When the school is calculating your expected contribution to their education costs, they will count about 5.6% of all investments held in your name as available to pay annual expenses. But the school will want up to 35% of the money in your child's name to be spent for tuition, housing, etc., each year, before they come up with any financial aid.

The difference is remarkable, as you can see in this example using $50,000 of assets, assuming a 6% annual return, and ignoring taxes and inflation:

Expected Annual Contribution Toward College Costs

	Money in Your Name	Money in Child's Name
Freshman year	$ 2,800	$17,500
Sophomore year	2,802	12,057
Junior year	2,805	8,307
Senior year	2,807	5,724
Extra senior year	2,807	3,943
Amount left at graduation	$47,351	$ 7,763

Almost $40,000 less of the assets would be counted on by the school.

Although dramatic, this example doesn't tell the whole story. Your child's aid package will likely include a lesser amount in grants and scholarships, and the gap between what money she has and what the cost actually is may be made up with loans. Conversely, just because the money is in your name doesn't mean you can't use it to pay your kid's college costs. But you may want to keep the money in your accounts until the school gives you their aid package.

Best Investments for an UTMA/UGMA Account

The factor you want to consider when deciding which vehicle is best for an UTMA/UGMA account is the potential tax liability. You obviously want the earnings to be taxed at the lowest rate possible, so you want to try to keep the annual interest, dividends, and capital gains to less than $1,500 per year, at least until your child turns fourteen.

1. Bonds If you don't mind the typically lower rate of return, zero coupon Treasury bonds (Chapter 7) can be a safe way to grow the money, as you would need almost $22,000 invested at 7% annually before the interest would be taxed at your top rate.

2. Mutual Funds and Common Stocks Index funds, tax-sensitive growth mutual funds (Chapter 1), and common stocks (Chapter 6) with little or no dividend are also a good choice until your child reaches fourteen. After that age, all income and gains will be taxed at her rate, which will likely be the lowest bracket.

Keep It in Your Name

So you want to do something for your child's future, but you are also concerned about the kid blowing the money.

Why not just keep it in your name?

Usually when I make this suggestion to parents who want to invest for their children, they look at me as if I don't quite understand what they want. "No, it's for our kids," they say. "It has to be in their names."

No, it doesn't.

I make the distinction between "gifting" cash or assets to your child's UTMA/UGMA account (and never getting the money back), as opposed to just designating or setting aside an account for the future benefit of your kid. If it helps you accept the concept, you can practice some "mental accounting" and title the account "(Your name), Children's Account," or something like that, and use your own Social Security number. And if you stick to the right investments, keeping the money in your name has some tremendous advantages.

Control

Unlike an UTMA/UGMA account that might give your child the money when she turns eighteen or twenty-one, you keep control over the asset forever. If your child is a toddler right now, that might not seem like a big deal. But you might be glad you kept the money in your name if your child goes through some years of "sowing her oats."

Once your child matures, settles down, and starts waking up around the time of day at which she used to come home, you can give her up to $10,000 per year in value with no gift tax (see Chapter 11), and your spouse can do the same. Don't necessarily sell the investment yourself, especially if you have a large, unrealized capital gain. Instead, give your child the asset, and let her sell it at her (likely) lower capital gains tax rate.

If your kid never reaches a suitable level of responsibility, you've got some extra money to splurge on yourself, or to donate to a worthy cause.

College Factor

As you saw in the UTMA/UGMA section, you can significantly lower the dollar amount of your family's expected contribution by keeping the money in your name.

If your income is in the six-figure range
(or higher), the best way to save for your
child's college education while keeping control of
the money is through the use of the Qualified State
Tuition Plans discussed in Chapter 2.

You can still use the assets to pay for your child's education.
However, you have to be careful that you don't liquidate any
holdings with large unrealized capital gains in the year or two
before your child enters college. If you do, these gains will arti-
ficially inflate your income, and will reduce the amount of aid
for which your child qualifies. You are better off selling the assets during your child's freshman or sophomore year of high
school, and parking the proceeds in a money market. The rate
earned there will be low, but the principal will be safe from the
ups and downs of the stock market.

Best Investments Kept in Your Name, for Your Child

**1. Common Stocks, Tax-Advantaged Mutual Funds, and Also
Index Funds** These investments usually generate little or no
annual capital gains or dividends, and therefore allow you to
keep most of your money working without paying high taxes.
Common growth stocks with low dividends will also keep
your tax bill low until you are ready to give your child the
money, and you can potentially save on the capital gains tax by
having your child sell the asset in her name.

2. Your Roth IRA Even if your own plan already meets your
retirement needs, don't overlook a Roth IRA for yourself or

your spouse. This vehicle is especially valuable if you are going to be 59½ or older by the time you would like your child to receive the money. And there are also significant advantages to making your child the beneficiary of your Roth IRA, and passing it to her upon your death (see Chapter 5).

3. Variable Annuity If you want to wait until you turn 59½ to give your child the money and you've already maxed out your IRA, Roth IRA, and 401(k) options, you may want to consider depositing money into a variable annuity (Chapter 4) in your own name. The good news is you still get the tax deferral on earnings, and the amount you can deposit into these accounts is virtually unlimited. But the downside is that you will have to pay tax on the withdrawals, and they will be taxed as ordinary income.

4. Tax-Free Bonds Finally, tax-free bonds kept in your name can be a great conservative investment for your child, especially zero coupon bonds (see Chapter 7). You don't add anything to your annual tax bill, and you can time the maturity of the bonds to match significant milestones in your child's life, like college, marriage, her first home, etc.

Trusts

I always thought the name "trust" was ironic, because trusts are best suited for parents who *don't* trust their kids to handle the money responsibly, at least not at age eighteen. These vehicles allow you to remove assets from your estate, and the income generated from your annual tax liability, just like an UTMA/UGMA account. Yet they also allow you to delay (or even deny) your kid's access to the funds, even after she turns eighteen. Depending on the type of trust you use and the language you incorporate, you can regulate your child's control over the money from the age of twenty-one all the way up to his retirement and old age, even from "beyond the grave"!

One of the disadvantages of giving your child money through a trust is the legal and administrative costs. You should plan on spending anywhere from a few hundred to a few thousand dollars to set up a trust, depending on the complexity of your instructions. There will also be ongoing annual expenditures, including trustee fees, tax preparation costs (you have to file a tax return for trusts each year), and any legal expenses or attorney fees. Therefore, you should pursue this course of action only if you expect the current or future value of the account to be at least in the tens of thousands of dollars.

Although you can structure a trust to meet your particular needs, if you want to still get access to the money, putting funds into an irrevocable trust is not for you. Once the money goes in, you can't take it back.

• • •

These negatives are usually outweighed by the significant tax and control benefits offered by most trusts. Wealthy benefactors have used these tools for over a century to remove taxable assets from their estates, provide for their current heirs, and make sure that money would be available for future generations. You can do the same, plus create your own customized "triggers" that allow for release of the funds.

Many parents who use trusts allow some or all of the principal to be withdrawn for these events in a child's adult life:

- Enrolling in college
- Graduating from college
- Getting married
- Starting a business
- Having a baby
- Retiring

I have one client who has established trusts for each of her children. She decided to allow the kids to gain access to the principal in parts, at various intervals of their respective lives.

The language in each trust agreement dictates that the child beneficiary will get one third of the account balance at the age of twenty-five, one half of the balance at thirty-five, and the remainder at age forty-five. If there is $75,000 in the account when the kid turns twenty-five and the money grows at 10% annually, the dollars distributed will look like this:

Child's Age	Payment
25	$ 25,000
35	64,843
45	168,188

We assume that the first payment will be wasted frivolously (and will be pleasantly surprised if it isn't), the second one will be spent a little more wisely, and by the time the third payment hits each child will be firmly entrenched in middle age, and will be staring straight into the face of retirement. If that doesn't inspire a little responsibility, nothing will.

You may wish to use a trust to encourage your child to work, and tie the release of funds to annual earnings. At the end of each year, your child could meet with the trustee and present proof of earnings. The trustee would then write a check for 50 cents for each dollar earned, until the trust was depleted. If your child has altruistic motives, you may want the trust to pay her for each hour worked at a charitable or nonprofit organization, especially if it is for a cause that's dear to you.

Finally, consider language in the trust that will allow the trustee to not release the principal, even if your child has reached the age or life achievement you originally intended to use as the trigger. Known as a "hold back" clause, this tool can keep your child's assets from being obliterated by chemical dependency, divorce, lawsuits, and bankruptcy.

You can set up a trust to address just about any goal or objective, but there are three trusts that allow you to contribute up to $10,000 each year (and your spouse can do the same) without incurring any gift tax: the 2503(b), the 2503(c), and the Crummey trust.

2503(b) Trust

This vehicle allows you to open a trust in your child's name (one trust per child). Your kid is the beneficiary, and you can use the annual exclusion to place up to $10,000 in the trust each year, as can your spouse. IRS regulations require that usually only a tiny portion of the gifted amount be counted as a taxable gift (it depends on current interest rates—an accountant or the IRS can tell you exactly what the percentage is). You can choose whatever age you wish for your child to gain access to some or all of the money. You can also designate certain things your child must achieve to receive the assets, like graduating from college, getting married, buying a house, etc.

Best Investments for a 2503(b) Trust

The only downfall of this trust is a requirement that all annual income from the trust be distributed to your child, and be taxed at her normal rates. This is not as bad as it sounds. First, while your child is a minor, any income can go from the trust to an UTMA/UGMA account in her name, which will allow you to delay her access to the accumulated interest until she reaches eighteen or twenty-one. Second, you can direct the trustee to purchase investments with a low probability of income payouts. Index funds, growth-oriented mutual funds, and common stocks with a growth objective should minimize the amount of money that your child can take out, whether as a minor or as an adult.

2503(c) Trust

This is the flip side to the 2503(b) trust. Again, you create one trust per child, and you (and your spouse) can gift up to $10,000 per year to the trust. The advantage over the previous trust is that all income can be kept within the trust, with no need to transfer it into an UTMA/UGMA account or give it directly to your child. And if you live in a state where a child takes control over an UTMA/UGMA account at age eighteen, you will be interested to know that a 2503(c) delays any access until the child turns twenty-one.

However, unlike the 2503(b), this trust might not necessarily be used to keep your child from taking control of the money until her twenties or thirties. Your kid can take all of the assets on her twenty-first birthday, and there is nothing you can do to stop her. You can, however, put language into the trust agreement that says she has a "window" of, say, thirty days after her twenty-first birthday, to withdraw the money. Whatever she doesn't remove stays in the 2503(c) trust, until whatever age you deem appropriate.

Best Investments for a 2503(c) Trust

Another tripping point of this type of trust is the taxation on income generated by the investments in the trust, and kept in the trust, especially for larger sums of money. Income *paid out* of this trust to your minor child is taxed at her rates.

	Under Fourteen	Over Fourteen
First $750	No tax	At her rate
Next $750	15% bracket	At her rate
Over $1,500	Your top bracket	At her rate

But for income retained in a 2503(c) trust, the income is taxed at trust rates, which go up in a hurry:

2001 Trust Tax Rates

Income	Rate
$0–1,800	15.0%
$1,801–4,250	27.5
$4,251–6,500	30.5
$6,501–8,900	35.5
$8,901–above	39.1

A 2503(c) trust holding $100,000 in Treasuries paying 7% interest would be taxed at the same top bracket as a child earning a six-figure income! Unless your kid is a teen pop music sensation, you will save a lot of tax dollars by either distributing the income to your child, or concentrating on tax-free bonds or tax-sensitive mutual funds.

Crummey Trust

If you don't like the mandatory annual income distributions of the 2503(b), or the required full distribution at twenty-one of the 2503(c), perhaps you should look at a Crummey trust. This unfortunately named vehicle arose out of a 1968 court battle between the IRS and the Crummey family.

The family's attorneys said the Crummeys could place an amount up to the annual exclusion from gift taxation ($10,000) in a trust for each of the Crummey children. The children had the right to withdraw the gift within thirty days of the deposit; if they didn't, the money stayed in the trust for as long as the parents wanted.

The IRS begged to differ, saying the money had to *always* be available to the children if it was going to count as a completed gift. Yet the Crummeys prevailed, and were rewarded with their trust document procedure being named in their honor, a pretty paltry prize for beating the IRS in court.

A Crummey trust is not a foolproof way to protect your child from derailing your plans to make her a millionaire. In essence, you are really giving her your annual deposit each year. You hope she will say, "No, thank you, please put the money in a trust so that it may grow to even larger amounts." The danger, of course, is that instead she will take the money and run.

There's not much you can do to stop her, but "fool me once, shame on you, fool me twice, shame on me" seems like an instructive axiom here. Don't give her any more money if you think she will repeat her disregard for her financial future. One advantage of a Crummey trust is that your child will only get a thirty-day window to convert the most recent deposit to her own use; all of the previous deposits and earnings will remain in the trust until the original language you wrote allows her to withdraw the funds.

Wouldn't it be easier to simply to make your deposits to the Crummey trust *without* first giving your kid notice that you are doing so? Of course it would, and that's why the IRS occasionally examines some of these instruments to make sure that the law is being followed. To comply with the regulations, whenever you want to deposit money into a Crummey trust, you should instruct your trustee to write a letter informing your child that she can take the funds. If you are a "belt *and* suspenders" kind of person you can go one step further and have your child sign a waiver, stating she agrees the deposit should go into the trust.

Best Investments for a Crummey Trust

As with the 2503(c) trust, keeping income in a Crummey trust can cause even a small amount of interest and dividends to be taxed at the highest rates. Therefore, you can best minimize the taxation with tax-free bonds, growth stocks, and mutual funds with little chance of an income distribution.

College Factor

All three of these trusts are looked at in the same manner by financial aid offices. The money will be considered part of your child's assets, and therefore up to 35% of the money will be figured into your family's annual expected contribution.

Getting Started

Deciding *why* you are investing is the first step to choosing how you are going to allow your child to gain access to the money. Spreading your money among UTMA accounts, trusts, and keeping it in your own name will allow the growth of the assets to parallel your child's growth, yet still make it possible for her to gain tangible experience and enjoyment from your benevolence.

chapter thirteen

Make Your Grandchild a Millionaire

Using So Little to Do So Much

At the risk of sounding like a greeting card, let's face it: being a grandparent is one of life's most extraordinary experiences. You are privileged to all the highlights of a child's life—watching him grow and develop, getting (and giving) love, and sharing in those monumental moments, from the first steps to the college graduation.

Yet, you are exempt from the day-to-day drudgery of raising a child and the dirty jobs of diapers and discipline. You've already paid your dues. Your job now is to spoil the kid, and don't think he's not aware of your position, either!

But as a grandparent, making that special child happy can go far beyond just cookies and candy. You also have a unique financial position in helping to make him rich (you knew I was getting to that, didn't you?).

Chances are you are moving from the "accumulation" phase of your life into the "preservation" or even "distribution" period. You probably have enough money to last your lifetime, and then some. Your children, on the other hand, might be having a hard enough time just making ends meet, let alone starting any long-term savings and investment plans for their children.

What's more, you realize how quickly time passes, and you know that planning ahead now will make tomorrow that much better for your future generations. By investing a few minutes of your time, not only can you help your grandchild realize his dreams and become financially independent, you can also save your family thousands of dollars in income and estate taxes.

The great news about investing for your grandchild is that regardless of your age or financial status, it doesn't take much money to make a difference. A few months of your Social Security checks deposited today can make a newborn grandchild a millionaire by the time he hits middle age (which, ironically enough, is about when those checks might *stop* going to retirees—one more reason that your actions today are so important to his future).

No matter what your age and income are, at least one of the following strategies will help you help your grandchild achieve a lifetime of opportunity and security.

Stretch Out Your IRA

One great way to provide for your grandchild tomorrow without cutting into your lifestyle today is to make him the beneficiary of your IRA. After you pass away, your retirement plan can be a potent tool to enrich your grandchild and cut your family's potential income tax bills for years to come.

Uncle Sam comes knocking on your door by April 1 of the year after you turn 70½, telling you to begin withdrawing money (your required minimum distribution) from your IRA so that he can tax it. You also have to choose your beneficiary by this date. You can choose your spouse as the beneficiary, and you obviously should if he or she is counting on the money as a source of support after you're gone.

But if nobody else will be relying on your IRA for financial assistance after you've died, you can choose a non-spouse, like your child or grandchild. Under rules put in place as of January

1, 2002, your choice of beneficiary doesn't affect your RMD. It is only after you've passed away that your choice of beneficiary matters.

This is because your beneficiary will be confronted with a choice of how he wants to take the money out. He can take it all out at once, but he will also pay a big chunk of income taxes on the withdrawal. Instead, what you hope he will do is recalculate the RMD based on his much-longer life expectancy, and take only the smallest amount allowed each year (which will probably then be taxed at a lower rate than a lump-sum distribution).

This option to withdraw the money slowly is especially important if the beneficiary is your grandchild. The younger the beneficiary is, the longer his life expectancy. The longer he is expected to live, the less he has to take out annually. The less he takes out, the more that can be left in the IRA, accumulating with no taxation.

Say you are seventy and have a $100,000 IRA, and you are going to live to be eighty. If the money earns 10% annually and you take out only the RMD each year, by the time you pass away the account will be worth about $180,000. Whoever you named as the beneficiary can now take all of the money out of the IRA. If he does, he has to pay income taxes on the withdrawal, which may be as much as 45% of the amount taken out.

But let's assume you named your wise little grandchild as the beneficiary when you were seventy and he was ten. If you pass away at age eighty, he will be twenty. His life expectancy at that point, according to the IRS, is 61.9 years, and he can stretch the annual RMD payments over that span. If he chooses to do so, and the money earns 10% annually, his annual income and ending balance will look like this at age sixty-five:

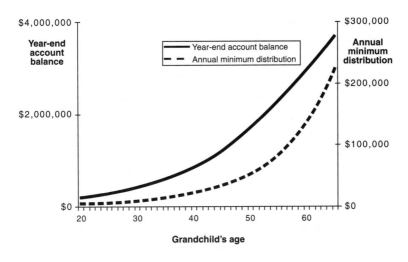

Grandchild's age

What a remarkable demonstration! Your grandchild would get income checks totaling around $2 million from the age of twenty to sixty-five, and would still have about $3.6 million left in the account when he turns sixty-five.

Multiple Grandchildren? If you want to provide for more than one grandchild, you have two options. First, you can make your grandchildren partial beneficiaries of your IRA, with a designated percentage share for each one.

The drawback to this is that after you have passed away, the IRS calculates the new annual RMD based only on the age of the oldest beneficiary. If your grandchildren's ages vary greatly from youngest to oldest, a single IRA shared by all of them will cause the money to be withdrawn more quickly than necessary.

A better solution is to split your IRA into several different accounts, one for each grandchild for whom you wish to provide. Then each child can determine the withdrawal rate that suits his situation, with no interference from the other grandkids. And the youngest ones aren't penalized by an RMD based on the age of a much older cousin (the same strategy also works great for your Roth IRA, described below).

Help Him Without Hurting Yourself The beauty of making a grandchild the beneficiary of your IRA is that not only can it save your family thousands of dollars in taxes, but it also provides maximum flexibility to you while you are alive. Although you hope to take out only the RMD each year, there is nothing to stop you from withdrawing more money if, say, you run into a streak of bad luck at the slot machines.

After your death, your grandchild will still be able to tailor his withdrawals to meet his changing needs. Theoretically, he will need to take out more money in years when his income is lower. A lower income will mean that the money is taxed at a lower bracket when it comes out. In his higher income years, he won't need as much money, so a lower amount will be taxed at the higher rates.

Trust Your Grandchild, or Use a Trust If you have a larger IRA and are concerned about putting too much money in the hands of an immature grandchild, you can create a trust that will collect the RMDs after you are gone (see Chapter 12). But this should be considered only if the value of the IRA will be in at least the six-figure range after your death; otherwise, the attorney and trustee expenses may not make the endeavor worthwhile.

Stretching Out a Roth IRA

Converting If you have an IRA, don't mind paying the taxes, and are eligible to convert the account to a Roth IRA, you can establish a cash generator for your grandchildren similar to the IRA example above.

Yet it will be even *better* than the regular IRA, because with an inherited Roth IRA, your grandchild will pay no federal taxes on the withdrawals. For example, in the above case your federal tax bill on converting a $100,000 Roth IRA might be around $25,000 to $35,000, depending on your tax bracket. But converting to a Roth IRA would save the grandchild in the example *millions* of dollars in federal taxes over his lifetime.

Another added benefit to your family is that the taxes that you pay on the conversion will immediately be removed from your estate, which might reduce the amount of estate taxes your family will have to pay.

And finally, once you convert your IRA to a Roth IRA, you don't have to make any government-mandated withdrawals at age 70½. And if you *have* begun making withdrawals, you can stop!

Contributing If you are still working, you can also make a current contribution to a Roth IRA, earmarking the account for your grandchild's future by making him the beneficiary.

Another way a Roth IRA is different from a regular IRA: You can still contribute to a Roth IRA past the age of 70½, as long as you have earned income at least equal to your contribution.

The tax laws enacted in 2001 not only allow for rising maximum contributions to IRAs and Roth IRAs (from $2,000 in 2001 to $5,000 in 2008), but there is a special provision that allows people over fifty to exceed the limits by $500 from 2002 to 2005, and $1,000 in 2006 and thereafter.

I know grandparents who take a small amount of money in payment for baby-sitting their grandchildren—this is the "earned income" needed to make a Roth IRA contribution—and then put an equal amount into a Roth IRA each year. They then make the grandchildren the beneficiaries of the Roth IRA. (You can learn more about converting and contributing to a Roth IRA in Chapter 5.)

You get to spend time with the grandkids, the parents get a trusted sitter to watch over their children, and your grandchildren could get hundreds of thousands of dollars of federally tax-free income over their lifetimes.

Now, there's a deal!

The Dynasty Trust

You should take a certain amount of pride in yourself if you've accumulated a decent-sized portfolio (into seven figures, not including the decimal point) by the autumn of your life. Hopefully, principal—and principles—will flow down through multiple layers of your descendants for decades to come.

Yet, good investing and disciplined saving are only half the battle. There are several other obstacles to your family's accumulating a fortune. Your progeny may need protection from impetuousness, poorly chosen spouses, and greedy lawyers. Thankfully, the trusts described in Chapter 12 go a long way to ensure that today's hard-earned dollars will survive these impediments to sustainable wealth.

However, because those trusts eventually allow the beneficiary to gain complete access to the principal of the trust, they don't fight the true enemy of your future generations' financial security: estate taxes.

Think ahead a few decades. Your children and your grandchildren have cultivated both your financial legacy and philosophy, and now sit on a small fortune in the tens of millions of dollars. If the money is in their respective names, and assuming estate taxes are still in existence in some form (a pretty good bet), the government might take up to half that fortune at the death of each generation.

The Rockefellers, Carnegies, and other ultrarich families are a few decades ahead of your family, both in terms of wealth creation, and solving the problems that come from wealth creation. For over a century many of these upper-crust clans have used some form of a Dynasty trust to provide for their offspring, yet defend against estate taxes.

Like most legal and estate planning strategies, implementing the Dynasty trust requires the help of a qualified attorney. But with the proper structure and a wise choice of the assets to be placed in the trust, you can turn a mid-five-figure expenditure into a hundred-million-dollar support system that lasts for a century or more.

Your first job is to set up the trust. The exact nature of the language in the trust agreement depends on the laws of the governing state. Many years ago the federal government realized that trusts that went on forever could provide ongoing income for the beneficiaries, without being subject to estate taxes. Laws against "perpetuity" were enacted, and now most states require that trusts terminate after a set period of time, usually no more than twenty-one years after the death of the last beneficiary living at the time the trust is created.

This can be a pretty long period, though. Say you create a trust for your grandchildren, the youngest of whom is now a toddler. She may live for another eighty years after the trust was started, and then the trust can still exist for up to twenty-one years after her death. This means the fruits of your efforts could last for over a hundred years before estate taxes would bite into the principal.

If the trust is established in the right state, your descendants can reap the benefits even longer. Over a dozen states, including Alaska, Delaware, Idaho, Illinois, South Dakota, and Wisconsin have either repealed their laws against perpetuity, or modified the existing laws to allow Dynasty trusts to last longer than they could in other states. And several others are considering either abolishing or curtailing their rules against Dynasty trusts. You don't necessarily even need to live in one of these states to create an income-producing vehicle that lasts forever.

If, after hearing the details of your specific circumstances, your attorney thinks you have the opportunity to create a never-ending Dynasty trust, direct the trustee to distribute only income and interest from the trust to your children, grandchildren, and beyond. This should leave the principal intact to grow indefinitely, generating still more income and interest.

Assuming your children will be provided for with assets outside the trust, you can extend the life of your trust by making your grandchildren the first generation of beneficiaries of a Dynasty trust. You can deposit over $1 million in a trust for your grandchildren. But any more than that will cause the Generation-Skipping Tax to kick in. The IRS uses this law to make sure it collects estate taxes at the death of *each* generation in a family, rather than every other one.

After you have established who the beneficiaries are, along with if (or when) they will have access to the principal, your final job is to fund the trust. Of course you can put just about any type of tangible asset in the trust, ranging from cash, stocks, and bonds, to real estate, antiques, and shares of a business. But you will probably get the biggest bang for the buck when you direct the trustee to purchase a life insurance policy on your life, owned by the trust. If you are concerned about the premiums being paid, you (and your spouse) can give up to your $10,000 annual exempt amounts to each of your grandchildren, who can then deposit the money in the trust. The trustee can then use these funds to buy as much whole life insurance as possible.

How much is enough? It depends on the magnitude of the dreams you have for your progeny. But considering the principal might grow for least 100 years before it is withdrawn by the beneficiaries, the amount you need today may not be as much as you think. Assuming the money earns 5% annually after taxes, and after any annual interest is distributed to the beneficiaries, a $500,000 amount paid to the trust by the insurance company at your death could be worth over $65 million a century later.

A One-Time Deposit for a Lifetime of Needs

A few years ago a couple called to share some great news. Their daughter had just given birth to their first grandchild, and the tone of their voices was elevated by their excitement. "We're calling you because we want to set up a fund for his college education," they said. "Let us know how much we need to deposit today to make sure that all of his costs will be taken care of."

As I hung up the phone, I began to assemble a standard package of investment options for them. I included the calculations as to what college might cost in twenty years, and how the rise in those expenses would compare with what they might earn on the deposit in the meantime. I sent the information out, and then met with them a few weeks later.

They said they were surprised by the numbers I gave them, and I launched into my speech about the inflation rate of tuition, blah, blah, blah. But they interrupted me and said, "No, the numbers you gave us were lower than we expected them to be. We have more than enough set aside to meet our grandchild's education needs. What else can we do for him?"

I thought about that for a moment. Paying for college is obviously the most important goal when we invest for children. But if that's covered, what other milestones will be important in this little boy's lifetime? "How about securing his retirement?" I said. "Come to think of it, you can help him buy a house, pay for a wedding, and maybe even have enough left over to get him a decent car for his sixteenth birthday."

This struck a nerve with them. They weren't megamillionaires, but they lived relatively simply and had more than enough to meet their needs. They also didn't expect to have many more grandchildren, so they could devote a decent portion of their assets to securing the future of the new joy in their lives. If you are in a similar situation financially and wish to meet all of your grandchild's financial obligations right now, you may be surprised how affordable it can be.

The Assumptions Before the costs can be figured, a little background. I'll use 6% annual inflation for college expenses, and 3% inflation for everything else. I'll also use a 10% annual rate of return for the investment accounts, since your grandchild's time horizon for these goals will be from eighteen to seventy years away, and you'll be able to invest with a long-term growth strategy in mind.

First off is the college education. I'll assume you are saving for a newborn grandchild (obviously the older the child in question, the more money that will need to be deposited). A degree from a public university today will set you back about $40,000. Eighteen years from now that same education might cost about $115,000. If you use a Section 529/Qualified State Tuition Plan (see Chapter 2), a deposit of $20,000 today should more than cover the expenses.

Then comes the wedding. You hope your grandchild will be the sensible sort who wouldn't blow a small fortune on a one-day event. But allowing for a little extravagance, $10,000 in today's dollars should cover a respectable contribution on your part. Assuming your grandchild will be married at age twenty-eight, a $2,000 deposit into a tax-efficient index mutual fund (see Chapter 1) or your Roth IRA (Chapter 5) should pay for enough powder blue tuxes and sea foam green bridesmaid dresses—trust me, they'll be back in fashion by then—yet still leave a little left over for a decent honeymoon.

A house can't be far behind the marriage, and may actually precede the event. A $150,000 house in today's dollars will cost around $350,000 thirty years from now. In the same fund you used for the wedding account an investment of $20,000 should pay for the whole house, or at least a good portion of it if your grandchild chooses to live in a higher-priced neighborhood.

Finally, retirement. I'll guess that the "normal" retirement age will be at least seventy by the time your grandchild gets there, and that he'll need at least $1 million in today's money to live comfortably. That's about $8 million seventy years from now, but a $10,000 deposit in a tax-deferred variable annuity (see Chapter 4) should get him to that level. And he'll have a paid-up house, plus the proceeds from his work-sponsored retirement plan, to make up for any shortfall.

Let's Go to the Tote Board The total of the deposits for a newborn baby will look like this:

Objective	Today's Deposit	Vehicle
College	$20,000	529/QSTP
Wedding	2,000	Index fund
House	20,000	Index fund
Retirement	10,000	Variable annuity
Total	$52,000	

That's about two years of larger Social Security checks, but it's not bad for taking care of *every single major expense* most people have over their lifetimes. As for the car on the sixteenth birthday, you can make that goal a little more sentimental. Whenever you're done with what you're driving today, park it in storage until your grandchild gets his license. When he does, clean up the car and give it to him. His friends will think it's a riot, and it will get him around until he can buy something other than what a middle-aged grandparent would choose to drive.

More Ideas Than You Have Grandchildren

Too many grandchildren, or not enough money to pay for all of the above goals? The following tips are ways you can apply information from other chapters of this book to help any number of grandchildren:

1. Variable Annuity (Chapter 4) If you have an existing annuity, and want to begin taking the money out, you can annuitize the account, taking monthly payments over the life expectancies of you and your grandchild. After your death, your grandchild will continue to receive a payment every year of his life, and only a small portion of it will be taxable. Of course, a small payment *into* an annuity in your grandchild's name will give him tax-deferred growth, with a 10% penalty on money he takes out before turning 59½. This (and the taxes) may serve as an incentive for him to leave the money in the account until he retires.

2. Life Insurance and a Will (Chapter 3) Talk to your child about the necessity of having a will and the proper amount of life insurance, especially if she has just become a new parent. Offer to recommend an attorney, pay the legal fees, and even pay the insurance premium if your child's budget is tight (the insurance premium is a good investment for you—if something were to happen to your child or her spouse, supporting your grandchild might cost you hundreds of thousands of dollars).

3. Common Stocks (Chapter 6) If you own common stocks with a large amount of unrealized capital gains and are thinking about selling them, consider gifting them to a grandchild over the age of fourteen (no more than $10,000 worth if you are single, and $20,000 if you're married). He can sell the stocks, and pay taxes based at his (likely) lower bracket.

4. College Expenses (Chapter 2) You have two opportunities to help your grandchild attend college, and at the same time get money out of your estate quickly. Usually you can give no more than $10,000 annually to your grandchild ($20,000 if given with your spouse), without eating into your exempt amount. But you can put up to $50,000 ($100,000 if you are married) into each of your grandchildren's Section 529/QSTP accounts immediately.

If you use the full $50,000 amount, you can't make any more contributions for five years, and if you die within five years of the deposit, only 20% per year elapsed since the deposit will qualify to be excluded from your estate. If your grandchild is already attending college, you can pay his tuition expenses directly to his qualified institution for any amount, and still not use up your $10,000 annual exemption.

5. Your Grandchild's Roth IRA (Chapter 8) If he is at least in his teens and not working, offer to pay him to do odd jobs around your house, and put the contributions into a Roth IRA in his name. If he is earning money from you or someone else but doesn't contribute to a Roth, you can make the contributions on his behalf.

6. Your Grandchild's 401(k) (Chapter 9) If he is working and has a qualified plan at work, find out if he is contributing the maximum amount allowed. If not, offer to subsidize his expenses so he can afford to put in as much as possible.

7. Your Grandchild's House (Chapter 10) You might have money in certificates of deposit at the local bank. Even if you charge below-market rates, you may be able to get a better return on your money by lending the funds to your grandchild to buy a house. And if your grandchild is going to live in your town, and you're thinking about getting *out* of your house, you can sell it to him in ways that benefit you both.

Getting Started

The first step to effectively providing for your grandchild's financial future is to talk to his parents. Tell them what you want to do (and why), and ask them if your idea is the best way they think you can help. They might have a goal that you weren't aware of, or an investment method that will meet your objectives more easily than the one you were planning on using. Even if they offer a suggestion that differs from your chosen method, you still have the right to put your money where you think best, and I doubt if they will turn you down!

If you are a recent inductee into the world of grandparent-hood, you may be wondering when and how much of your money you should give to your grandchild. Excitement and pride may tempt you to go overboard in securing his financial future. But if you are in your late fifties or early sixties and only of moderate means, you should resist the urge to transfer too much money right now, for the following reasons:

- The National Center for Health Statistics says 26% of people who turned sixty-five in the year 2000 are expected to live until the age of ninety. You might have another forty years of life in which you aren't working but still have to support yourself.
- You probably have benefited greatly from the economic boom of the past decade or so. But booms can go bust, and you don't want to be stuck in retirement with not enough money and a declining investment portfolio.
- Giving money to your grandchild makes good tax sense, as the first $750 of annual earnings on his money is tax-free and the next $750 is taxed at his low rate. But until he is fourteen, anything over $1,500 is taxed at his parents' rate, which may be substantially higher than yours. Once your grandchild's annual interest and dividends approach that $1,500 level, or until he reaches the age of fourteen, you are better off keeping the money in your name, assuming your bracket is lower than your children's.
- You don't know how many grandchildren you will end up with, and you don't want to give any of them less than the others, just because they were born later.

Once you have reached your seventies and eighties you will have a stronger incentive to give away larger amounts because:

- You will be less likely to use up the assets you have accumulated, and can afford to give more away.
- You may be trying to reduce the size of your portfolio to avoid heavy estate taxation upon your death.
- You may wish to reduce your assets to a level that may qualify for Medicare assistance for potential nursing home expenses.
- You have a better idea on the number of grandchildren for whom you are providing, and their respective characters.

Some Advice on Getting Advice

Can you achieve your child's financial independence on your own?

Definitely. Millions of people (many of them not *nearly* as smart as you) have invested their money, done their taxes, and even written their own wills without any help from a financial adviser, accountant, or attorney.

Should you, too?

That depends on a couple of things.

The first factor is how interested and skilled you are in handling financial matters yourself. I don't get excited by the idea of a do-it-myself home improvement project, for example. I would rather pay someone else and make sure the job gets done right.

But I also don't disparage the legions of people lined up at Home Depot on a Saturday morning. If anything, I envy the enthusiasm they have for saving a little money and getting the satisfaction of working with their hands to make their home a better place for their family.

The second factor that will determine whether you should hire an adviser is the complexity of your situation. Like working around your house, the difficulty of the financial planning process varies (although Rachel discourages me from using power tools, she will occasionally allow me to hang a picture frame if I wear safety glasses and a hard hat).

Every chapter in this book gives you plenty of detailed instruction to get you started, and to finish the process of investing at the various stages of your child's life. However, a few issues (such as estate planning and establishing trusts) should only be completed with the help of a professional.

Does My Dependent Child Need to File a Tax Return?

Under most circumstances, you need to file a tax return for your dependent child if you can answer "yes" to any of the following questions:

1. Did she have more than $750 of unearned income (for 2001)?
2. Did she have earned income greater than the standard deduction ($4,550 for 2001)?
3. Add her unearned income to her earned income. Is the total more than the greater of

   • $750 (for 2001), or
   • Her earned income plus $250, up to the standard deduction ($4,550 for 2001)?

4. Did she earn more than $400 from odd jobs? (She won't owe income taxes, but she may be liable for self-employment taxes.)

Index

About the Author

Kevin McKinley is a Certified Financial Planner practitioner and Vice President–Investments at a large financial services firm. His practice and speaking engagements are focused on helping families achieve multigenerational wealth. He lives in Eau Claire, Wisconsin, with his wife and daughter.